Dreamweaver CS3: Advanced

Student Manual

ACE Edition

Dreamweaver CS3: Advanced

President & Chief Executive Officer:	Michael Springer
Vice President, Product Development:	Adam A. Wilcox
Vice President, Operations:	Josh Pincus
Director of Publishing Systems Development:	Dan Quackenbush
Writer:	Steve English
Developmental Editor:	Brandon Heffernan
Series Designer:	Adam A. Wilcox

Trademarks

ILT Series is a trademark of Axzo Press.

Some of the product names and company names used in this book have been used for identification purposes only and may be trademarks or registered trademarks of their respective manufacturers and sellers.

Disclaimers

We reserve the right to revise this publication and make changes from time to time in its content without notice.

The Adobe Approved Certification Courseware logo is either a registered trademark or trademark of Adobe Systems Incorporated in the United States and/or other countries. The Adobe Approved Certification Courseware logo is a proprietary trademark of Adobe. All rights reserved.

The ILT Series is independent from ProCert Labs, LLC and Adobe Systems Incorporated, and are not affiliated with ProCert Labs and Adobe in any manner. This publication may assist students to prepare for an Adobe Certified Expert exam, however, neither ProCert Labs nor Adobe warrant that use of this material will ensure success in connection with any exam.

Student Manual
ISBN-10: 1-4260-9721-2_1-4260-9723-9
ISBN-13: 978-1-4260-9721-8

Student Manual with data CD
ISBN-10: 1-4260-9723-9
ISBN-13: 978-1-4260-9723-2

Printed in the United States of America

1 2 3 4 5 6 7 8 9 10 GL 11 10 09

Contents

Introduction

After reading this introduction, you'll know how to:

A Use ILT Series manuals in general.

B Use prerequisites, a target student description, course objectives, and a skills inventory to set your expectations properly for the course.

C Re-key this course after class.

Topic A: About the manual

ILT Series philosophy

Our manuals facilitate your learning by providing structured interaction with the software itself. While we provide text to explain difficult concepts, the hands-on activities are the focus of our courses. By paying close attention as your instructor leads you through these activities, you'll learn the skills and concepts effectively.

We believe strongly in the instructor-led class. During class, focus on your instructor. Our manuals are designed and written to facilitate your interaction with your instructor and not to call attention to manuals themselves.

We believe in the basic approach of setting expectations, delivering instruction, and providing summary and review afterwards. For this reason, lessons begin with objectives and end with summaries. We also provide overall course objectives and a course summary to provide both an introduction to and closure on the entire course.

Manual components

The manuals contain these major components:

- Table of contents
- Introduction
- Units
- Appendix
- Course summary
- Quick reference
- Glossary
- Index

Each element is described below.

Table of contents

The table of contents acts as a learning roadmap.

Introduction

The introduction contains information about our training philosophy and our manual components, features, and conventions. It contains target student, prerequisite, objective, and setup information for the specific course.

Units

Units are the largest structural component of the course content. A unit begins with a title page that lists objectives for each major subdivision, or topic, within the unit. Within each topic, conceptual and explanatory information alternates with hands-on activities. Units conclude with a summary comprising one paragraph for each topic, and an independent practice activity that gives you an opportunity to practice the skills you've learned.

The conceptual information takes the form of text paragraphs, exhibits, lists, and tables. The activities are structured in two columns, one telling you what to do, the other providing explanations, descriptions, and graphics.

Appendix

The appendix for this course lists the Adobe Certified Expert (ACE) exam objectives for Dreamweaver CS3, along with references to corresponding coverage in Course ILT courseware.

Course summary

This section provides a text summary of the entire course. It's useful for providing closure at the end of the course. The course summary also indicates the next course in this series, if there is one, and lists additional resources you might find useful as you continue to learn about the software.

Quick reference

The quick reference is an at-a-glance job aid summarizing some of the more common features of the software.

Glossary

The glossary provides definitions for all of the key terms used in this course.

Index

The index at the end of this manual makes it easy for you to find information about a particular software component, feature, or concept.

Manual conventions

We've tried to keep the number of elements and the types of formatting to a minimum in the manuals. This approach aids in clarity and makes the manuals more elegant looking. But there are some conventions and icons you should know about.

Item	Description
Italic text	In conceptual text, indicates a new term or feature.
Bold text	In unit summaries, indicates a key term or concept. In an independent practice activity, indicates an explicit item that you select, choose, or type.
`Code font`	Indicates code or syntax.

`Longer strings of ►`
`    code will look ►`
`    like this.`
	In the hands-on activities, any code that's too long to fit on a single line is divided into segments by one or more continuation characters (►). This code should be entered as a continuous string of text.

Select **bold item**	In the left column of hands-on activities, bold sans-serif text indicates an explicit item that you select, choose, or type.
Keycaps like (↵ ENTER)	Indicate a key on the keyboard you must press.

Hands-on activities

The hands-on activities are the most important parts of our manuals. They're divided into two primary columns. The "Here's how" column gives short instructions to you about what to do. The "Here's why" column provides explanations, graphics, and clarifications. Here's a sample:

Do it!

A-1: Creating a commission formula

Here's how	Here's why
1 Open Sales	This is an oversimplified sales compensation worksheet. It shows sales totals, commissions, and incentives for five sales reps.
2 Observe the contents of cell F4	`F4  ▼   =  =E4*C_Rate`
	The commission rate formulas use the name "C_Rate" instead of a value for the commission rate.

For these activities, we've provided a collection of data files designed to help you learn each skill in a real-world business context. As you work through the activities, you'll modify and update these files. Of course, you might make a mistake and therefore want to re-key the activity starting from scratch. To make it easy to start over, you'll rename each data file at the end of the first activity in which the file is modified. Our convention for renaming files is to add the word "My" to the beginning of the file name. In the above activity, for example, a file called "Sales" is being used for the first time. At the end of this activity, you'd save the file as "My sales," thus leaving the "Sales" file unchanged. If you make a mistake, you can start over using the original "Sales" file.

In some activities, however, it might not be practical to rename the data file. If you want to retry one of these activities, ask your instructor for a fresh copy of the original data file.

Topic B: Setting your expectations

Properly setting your expectations is essential to your success. This topic will help you do that by providing:

- Prerequisites for this course
- A description of the target student
- A list of the objectives for the course
- A skills assessment for the course

Course prerequisites

Before taking this course, you should be familiar with personal computers and the use of a keyboard and a mouse. Furthermore, this course assumes that you've completed the following courses or have equivalent experience:

- *Dreamweaver CS3: Basic, ACE Edition*

Target student

This course will benefit students who want to learn how to use Dreamweaver CS3 to create and modify Web sites. You'll learn how to define content sections and apply CSS styles, manage site assets, create interactive forms, apply AP div tags and behaviors, add multimedia files, and integrate XML-based data and transform XML with XSLT. You should have prior experience with Dreamweaver, including formatting text, creating tables, applying images and links, managing Web site files, and publishing a site.

Adobe ACE certification

This course is designed to help you pass the Adobe Certified Expert (ACE) exam for Dreamweaver CS3. For complete certification training, you should complete this course and the following:

- *Dreamweaver CS3: Basic, ACE Edition*

Course objectives

These overall course objectives will give you an idea about what to expect from the course. It's also possible that they'll help you see that this course isn't the right one for you. If you think you either lack the prerequisite knowledge or already know most of the subject matter to be covered, you should let your instructor know that you think you are misplaced in the class.

Note: In addition the general objectives listed below, specific ACE exam objectives are listed at the beginning of each topic (where applicable). For a complete mapping of ACE objectives to Course ILT content, see Appendix A.

After completing this course, you'll know how to:

- Identify advantages of using CSS and the difference between internal and external style sheets; link a page to an external style sheet; define content sections with <div> tags and IDs; and edit CSS rules.

- Create and update library items and snippets; create and edit server-side includes; create page templates, define editable regions, and apply templates to other site pages; create and edit head elements; and add keywords and descriptions to pages.

- Create an interactive form and add a variety of input components to it, and set the tab order of form fields.

- Create a navigation bar using rollover images, and use behaviors to swap images on the page and to open a new browser window, and download Dreamweaver extensions.

- Insert AP Divs by using the Draw AP Div tool; manipulate the position, size, and visibility of AP Divs; and control visibility dynamically.

- Insert Flash buttons and Flash text, add Flash and FlashPaper files to Web pages, add Windows Media Player files and QuickTime files, and create basic animation using the Timelines panel.

- Convert an HTML page to an XSLT page, bind XML data to an XSLT page, create a repeat region in an XSLT page, create dynamic links, and attach an XSLT page to an XML document.

- Use Check In/Check Out options, use Design Notes to manage files in a group work setting, check for browser-specific errors using the Check Browser Compatibility feature, and check for and fix accessibility problems.

Skills inventory

Use the following form to gauge your skill level entering the class. For each skill listed, rate your familiarity from 1 to 5, with five being the most familiar. *This isn't a test.* Rather, it's intended to provide you with an idea of where you're starting from at the beginning of class. If you're wholly unfamiliar with all the skills, you might not be ready for the class. If you think you already understand all of the skills, you might need to move on to the next course in the series. In either case, you should let your instructor know as soon as possible.

Skill	1	2	3	4	5
Linking pages to external style sheets					
Defining document sections					
Editing CSS rules					
Creating and applying ID styles					
Creating, placing, and updating library items					
Creating and using snippets					
Creating, placing, and updating server-side includes					
Creating, applying, and updating page templates					
Editing head elements					
Defining keywords and descriptions for a site					
Creating a form					
Inserting form input fields					
Controlling the tab order of input fields					
Creating a navigation bar with rollover images					
Applying the Swap Image behavior					
Downloading Dreamweaver extensions					
Inserting and manipulating AP Divs					
Controlling AP Div visibility					
Inserting Flash elements (Flash buttons and text)					
Inserting multimedia content (FlashPaper content and movie files)					
Creating timeline animation					

Skill	1	2	3	4	5
Converting an HTML page to an XSLT page					
Binding XML data to an XSLT page					
Creating a repeat region in an XSLT page					
Creating a dynamic link in an XSLT page					
Attaching an XSLT page to an XML page					
Checking files in and out					
Adding Design notes					
Checking for browser-specific errors					
Checking for and fixing accessibility problems					

Topic C: Re-keying the course

If you have the proper hardware and software, you can re-key this course after class. This section explains what you need in order to do so and how to do it.

Hardware requirements

Your personal computer should have:

- A keyboard and a mouse
- Intel® Pentium® 4 or equivalent processor
- 512 MB RAM
- 1 GB of hard-disk space
- A DVD-ROM drive for installation
- An XGA monitor with 1024×768 resolution and 24-bit color support

Software requirements

You need the following software:

- Microsoft® Windows® XP with Service Pack 2 or Windows Vista™ Home Premium, Business, Ultimate, or Enterprise (certified for 32-bit editions); updated with the most recent service packs
- Dreamweaver CS3
- Microsoft Word 2000, XP, 2003, or 2007 (Required to complete Activity C-2 in the unit titled, "Site assets".)

Network requirements

The following network components and connectivity are also required for this course:

- Internet access, for the following purposes:
    - Updating the Windows operating system at update.microsoft.com.
    - Downloading and installing QuickTime. (Required to complete activity B-4 in the unit titled, "Multimedia.")
    - Downloading the Student Data files (if necessary)

Setup instructions to re-key the course

Before you re-key the course, you need to perform the following steps.

1   Download the latest critical updates and service packs from www.windowsupdate.com.

2   From the Control Panel, open the Display Properties dialog box and apply the following settings:

- Theme — Windows XP
- Screen resolution — 1024 by 768 pixels
- Color quality — High (24 bit) or higher

If you choose not to apply these display settings, your screens might not match the screen shots in this manual.

3   If necessary, reset any Dreamweaver CS3 defaults that you've changed. If you don't wish to reset the defaults, you can still re-key the course, but some activities might not work exactly as documented. For example, your workspace might show different panels or panel groups.

4   Adjust Internet properties as follows:

     a   Start Internet Explorer. Choose Tools, Internet Options.

     b   On the General tab, click Use Blank, and click Apply.

     c   On the Advanced tab, under Security, check Allow active content to run in files on My Computer, and click Apply. (This option appears only if you updated Windows XP with Service Pack 2.)

     d   On the Connections tab, click Setup to start the Internet Connection Wizard.

     e   Click Cancel. A message box appears.

     f   Check "Do not show the Internet Connection wizard in the future" and click Yes.

     g   Close the Internet Options dialog box, and close Internet Explorer.

5   Display file extensions.

     a   Start Windows Explorer.

     b   Choose Tools, Folder Options and select the View tab.

     c   Clear the check box for Hide extensions for known file types.

     d   Close Windows Explorer.

6   Create a folder named Student Data at the root of the hard drive. For a standard hard drive setup, this will be C:\Student Data.

7   Download the student data files for the course. (If you don't have an Internet connection, you can ask your instructor for a copy of the data files on a disk.)

     a   Connect to www.axzopress.com.

     b   Under Downloads, click Instructor-Led Training.

     c   Browse the subject categories to locate your course. Then click the course title to display a list of available downloads. (You can also access these downloads through our Catalog listings.)

     d   Click the link(s) for downloading the Student Data files, and follow the instructions that appear on your screen.

8   Copy the data files to the Student Data folder.

CertBlaster software

CertBlaster pre- and post-assessment software is available for this course. To download and install this free software, complete the following steps:

1   Go to www.axzopress.com.
2   Under Downloads, click CertBlaster.
3   Click the link for Dreamweaver CS3.
4   Save the .EXE file to a folder on your hard drive. (**Note**: If you skip this step, the CertBlaster software will not install correctly.)
5   Click Start and choose Run.
6   Click Browse and then navigate to the folder that contains the .EXE file.
7   Select the .EXE file and click Open.
8   Click OK and follow the on-screen instructions. When prompted for the password, enter **c_dwCS3**.

Unit 1

CSS layout

Unit time: 50 minutes

Complete this unit, and you'll know how to:

A Identify the advantages of using CSS and the difference between internal and external style sheets.

B Link a page to an external style sheet, define content sections with <div> tags and IDs, and edit CSS rules.

Topic A: Overview of style sheets

CSS

Explanation

By itself, HTML provides limited design capability. Browsers apply default styles to many elements, such as headings, paragraphs, block quotes, and tables, but these default styles are typically not enough to achieve the design you have in mind. *Cascading Style Sheets (CSS)* is the standard style language for the Web, and you can use it to control every aspect of your Web site's appearance. CSS and HTML work together; HTML provides the basic structure, and CSS controls how the elements within that structure appear in a browser. You can also use CSS to augment your document structure.

Style sheet types

You can apply CSS styles by using *internal style sheets* or *external style sheets*. Both style sheet types use the same syntax; the decision to use an internal or external style sheet depends on whether the style applies only to a single page, or to an element or elements on several pages.

Internal style sheets

An internal style sheet is embedded inside a page's head section, and the style rules it contains apply only to that page. You should use an internal style sheet when you know that a style is needed on that one page only.

External style sheets

An external style sheet is a text file that contains CSS rules and is saved with a .css extension. You can link an unlimited number of pages to an external style sheet, which provides a great deal of control and efficiency. Advantages to using external style sheets include:

- If your Web site consists of hundreds of pages, and you want the text formatting to be consistent, you can create a single rule in an external style sheet, and all pages linked to that style sheet will use the same formatting attributes. If you ever need to change formatting, you can change a single rule, rather than having to update hundreds of pages separately.

- It reduces the overall file size of your Web site, because all your style definitions are in a single location, rather than duplicated on every page. The smaller the file size of your pages, the faster those pages load in a browser.

- It allows you to separate your style information from your content and structure. This makes your Web site more efficient, easier to maintain, and easier for search engines to index.

- The ability to control the design of multiple pages from a single style sheet saves development and maintenance time and helps prevent errors and inconsistencies.

You can also use internal and external style sheets at the same time. You can place all your global styles (those that apply to multiple pages) in an external style sheet, and you can place your page-specific styles in internal style sheets.

Conflict resolution: The cascade

If conflicts arise, the styles in the internal style sheet take precedence. For example, if a rule in an external style sheet declares that all level-one headings should be blue, and a rule in a page's internal style sheet declares that all level-one headings should be green, the level-one headings in that page only will be green, while the headings of other pages will be unaffected and remain blue, in accordance with the rule in the external style sheet. The cascading part of Cascading Style Sheets refers to the way style sheets resolve these types of style conflicts. The general rule is this: The closer the style declaration is to the element that is to be styled, the more weight is given the rule. Also, the more specific the rule (the more specific the selector in use), the more weight is given to that rule. This is referred to as *specificity*.

CSS media type support

You can develop content for various types of media. For example, in addition to Web content, you might need to display information on handheld devices or in print. Use CSS to control attributes for each media type, and then preview the content in Dreamweaver. When a style sheet contains code that directs browsers or other media devices to specific rules within the sheet, it's called a *media-dependent style sheet*. For more information about media-dependent style sheets, visit the W3C site at `www.w3.org/TR/CSS21/media.html`.

If you're using a media-dependent style sheet, you can render your pages for various media types using the Style Rendering toolbar, shown in Exhibit 1-1. By default, the toolbar is hidden. To open it, choose View, Toolbars, Style Rendering. Click the media type buttons to render the content.

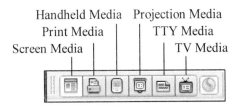

Exhibit 1-1: The Style Rendering toolbar

Do it!

A-1: Discussing style sheets

Questions and answers

1 How do HTML and CSS work together?

2 If you wanted to apply a style to an element on one page only, should you use an internal or external style sheet? Why?

3 What are some advantages of using an external style sheet?

4 In your own development work, do you think you'll use more internal or external style sheets, or both? Why?

5 A rule in an external style sheet declares that all paragraphs should have a font size of 12 pixels. A page linked to that style sheet also contains an internal style sheet that declares that all paragraphs should be 11 pixels. What will be the resulting font size of paragraphs on this particular page?

Topic B: Page layout

This topic covers the following Adobe ACE exam objectives for Dreamweaver CS3.

#	Objective
1.1	Given an HTML tag, explain the purpose of that tag.
2.12	Given a scenario, choose the proper method to lay out a page.
1.2	Describe the difference between CSS classes and IDs.
3.4	Create and maintain Cascading Style Sheets (CSS.)

Layout options

The easiest way to create Web pages is to use the CSS starter pages provided by Dreamweaver. If necessary, you can adapt them to your needs. If you decide to lay out your own pages, there are several methods from which to choose. You can use tables, AP Div tags, or the CSS Box model.

Using tables

For a basic Web page that won't require much updating, an HTML table can provide a quick and easy way to establish a page layout. However, there are disadvantages to using tables. Tables require a lot of code, which can make a file unnecessarily large. This code can also be difficult to modify, depending on the complexity of the layout table.

Use <div> tags to define content sections

A more efficient way to establish a page layout is to use <div> tags and CSS. The <div> (division) tag acts as a generic container for page elements. You can use it to define major content sections, such as navigation bars, content sections, headers, and footers, and you can give each section a logically named ID to augment your document structure. You can then apply styles to each ID, and all elements within each division will be formatted as a group.

For example, Exhibit 1-2 shows the code used to define a column of content in a layout. All the page elements included in the column are wrapped in <div> tags, which format the elements in the column as a single object. You use the column's ID ("columnLeft") to apply CSS styles to the section.

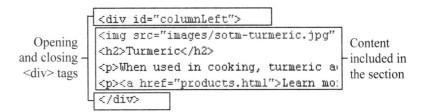

Exhibit 1-2: An example of content wrapped within <div> tags

Do it!

B-1: Discussing page layout options

Questions and answers
1 What are some advantages to using Div tags and CSS to create a page layout?
2 What are some disadvantages to using tables for page layout?
3 What's the function of a Div tag?
4 You're creating a large Web site that will be updated regularly and maintained by several developers. Which layout method should you use, tables or <div> tags with CSS? Why?

Linking pages to an external style sheet

When you're working with content sections that are used on multiple pages, such as navigation bars and copyright footers, you should enter the style rules in an external style sheet, rather than in individual internal style sheets, for each applicable page. Think of an external style sheet as a repository for all of your site's global styles. If multiple pages need the style, it belongs in an external style sheet. Then, link the appropriate pages to the style sheet. When you update a style in the external style sheet, it affects all of the pages linked to it.

An external style sheet must be saved with a .css extension. To attach an existing style sheet to a Web page:

1 Open a Web page.
2 In the CSS Styles panel, click the Attach Style Sheet button. The Attach External Style Sheet dialog box opens.
3 Click Browse and navigate to the CSS file.
4 Select the CSS file and click OK.
5 Click OK.

Do it!

B-2: Linking a page to an external style sheet

Here's how	Here's why
1 Start Dreamweaver CS3	Choose Start, All Programs, Adobe Dreamweaver CS3.
2 Choose **Site, New Site...**	To open the Site Definitions dialog box. You'll create a new site in the current unit folder.
3 Activate the Advanced tab	If necessary.
Edit the Site name box to read **Outlander CSS**	
In the Local root folder box, open and select the Outlander folder	Click the folder icon. Navigate to the current unit folder, open the Outlander folder, and click Select.
4 In the Category list, select **Remote Info**	
In the Access list, verify that **None** is selected	
Click **OK**	To create the site. Dreamweaver displays the site in the Files panel.
5 Open index.html	(In the Files panel, double-click index.html.) You'll attach a style sheet to this page.
Switch to Code view	In the Document toolbar, click the Code button.
Locate the head section	There is currently no external style sheet linked to the page.
6 Activate the CSS Styles panel	(If necessary.) You'll attach a style sheet to the page.
7 Click [icon]	(The Attach Style Sheet button is at the bottom of the CSS Styles panel.) The Attach External Style Sheet dialog box opens.
Click **Browse**	To open the Select Style Sheet File dialog box.
Navigate to the styles folder and select **globalstyles.css**	(The styles folder is inside the Outlander folder, in the current unit folder.) This external style sheet contains existing styles.
Click **OK**	To select the style sheet.

8 Verify that **Link** is selected	(In the Attach External Style Sheet dialog box.) The styles will be linked, rather than embedded in the document as an internal style sheet.
Click **OK**	
Observe the head section	(In Code view.) A link to the style sheet appears in the head section.
9 Switch to Design view	To preview the changes. Some of the text is formatted, but the overall layout of the page is disorganized.
10 Save the page	You'll continue to work on this page in the next activity.

Document sections

Most Web pages are divided into sections, as illustrated in Exhibit 1-3. For example, many Web pages have a banner or a navigation bar at the top of the page and then, perhaps, several columns of information below.

Dividing a layout into distinct sections makes it easier to arrange each section on the page and control styles within each section. If you use the same basic page layout for multiple pages, as most Web sites do, defining separate content sections is vital to a consistent and efficient layout. Controlling a layout with CSS is efficient, because the style and positioning rules are stored in a style sheet that's shared by multiple pages. Therefore, less code is required to achieve a particular layout and there's no need for duplication across pages. You use `<div>` tags to define document sections.

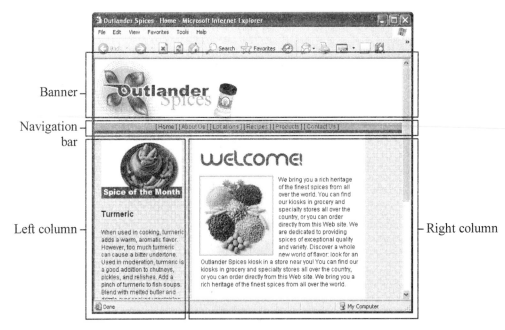

Exhibit 1-3: An example of a page divided into distinct sections

Applying <div> tags

You can create a new, empty <div> container and add content to it, or you can create a <div> to enclose existing content. When inserting a <div> tag, you might find it easier to work in Code view for precise placement of the insertion point. You can also enter the code manually, if you prefer.

To create a new <div> tag section:

1 (Optional) View the page in Code view.

2 Place the insertion point where you want the <div> tag to begin.

3 On the Insert bar, click the Insert Div Tag button. The Insert Div Tag dialog box opens, as shown in Exhibit 1-4.

4 In the Insert list, verify that At insertion point is selected.

5 (Optional) Select a Class or ID to apply to the tag. (If no existing class or ID styles exist, these dropdown lists are empty.)

6 Click OK.

7 Delete the sample text that Dreamweaver inserts in the <div> tag.

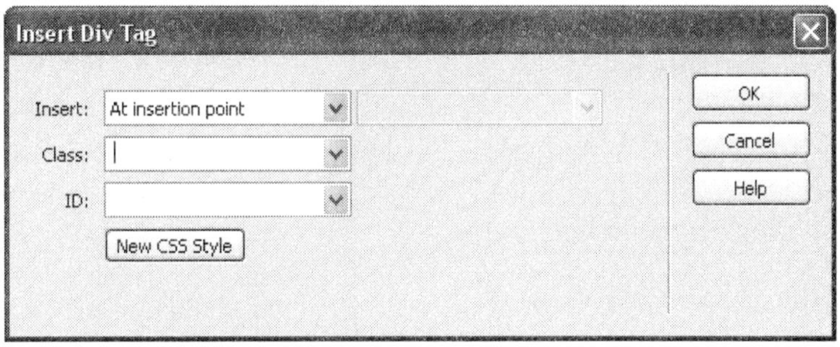

Exhibit 1-4: The Insert Div Tag dialog box

To wrap a <div> tag around existing content:

1 Select the content in Code view or Design view.

2 On the Insert bar, click Insert Div Tag. The Insert Div Tag dialog box opens.

3 In the Insert list, verify that Wrap around selection is selected.

4 (Optional) Select a Class or ID.

5 Click OK.

Applying a class or ID to a <div> tag

If you want to apply a class style or ID style to a <div> section, you can create the style first, so that you can select it from the Class or ID list in the Insert Div Tag dialog box. If you haven't yet created the style you want, you can open the Insert Div Tag dialog box and click New CSS Style to define a new class or ID style.

Do it!

B-3: Defining document sections

Here's how	Here's why
1 Switch to Code view	
2 Locate the HTML comments	Comments are notes that you can insert into the code to help make it easier to read and understand and to locate particular code blocks. Comments don't appear in a browser, and appear as gray text in Code view.
3 Place the insertion point in the masthead section, as shown	

```
11
12        <!-- Begin masthead secti
13  <a href="index.html">home</a>
    locations</a> | <a href="prod
    href="mailto:info@outlandersp
```

You'll insert a `<div>` tag that will hold the Outlander logo.

Here's how	Here's why
4 Switch to Split view	To view both Code and Design view.
In the Insert bar, click [icon]	(The Insert Div Tag button.) To open the Insert Div Tag dialog box.
From the ID list, select **logo**	This existing style sets the Outlander logo as a background image. Later, you'll examine the style more closely.
Click **OK**	Dreamweaver automatically inserts some placeholder text in the `<div>`.
5 Press (DELETE)	To Delete the placeholder text.
6 Click the logo in Design view	To refresh Design view. The logo appears at the top of the page. The `<div>` tag you inserted has an ID named "logo." The existing logo style sets logo.gif as the background of the `<div>` tag.
7 Why might you want to insert an image with a style sheet?	

8 In the masthead section, select the indicated code

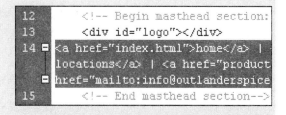

```
12        <!-- Begin masthead section:
13        <div id="logo"></div>
14 ⊟ <a href="index.html">home</a> |
     locations</a> | <a href="product
   ⊟ href="mailto:info@outlanderspice
15        <!-- End masthead section-->
```

You'll enclose the existing content (the navigation links) in a new <div> section.

Click the Insert Div Tag button

Observe the Insert list

Because you selected a block of code, Dreamweaver automatically selects Wrap around selection.

From the ID list, select **globalNav**

Click **OK**

Dreamweaver wraps a <div> tag with the id "globalNav" around the selection.

9 Select all the code between the left column comments, as shown

```
19        <!-- Begin left column sect:
20 ⊟ <img src="images/sotm-turmeric.
     >
21    <h2>Turmeric</h2>
22    <p>When used in cooking, turmer:
     cause a bitter undertone.</p>
23 ⊟ <p><a href="products.html">Lear
24        <!-- End left column sectior
```

You'll make this content appear on the left side of the page.

Wrap the selection in a <div> and apply the ID **columnLeft**

In Design view, you can see that some of the content overlaps. You'll fix this by applying <div> tags that format the remaining content into columns.

10 Select all the code between the
center column comments

```
27        <!-- Begin center column se
28 ▭ <img src="images/outlander_chic
   "imageRight" />
29   <h1>Try this recipe</h1>
30   <h2>Outlander Chicken</h2>
31   <p> This dish goes well with a
   chili powder and coriander give
32   <p>This recipe is available in
33   <p><a href="recipes.html">Click
34   <h1>Hungry for more Outlander r
35   <p> Sign up to have them delive
   weeks, guaranteed to add some s
36 ▭ <p><a href="inforequest.html">A
37        <!-- End center column sect
```

Wrap the selection in a `<div>` and
apply the ID **columnCenter**

11 Select all the code between the
right column comments

```
40        <!-- Begin right column sect
41 ▭ <h1>Did you know?</h1>
42   <p>Recent studies have shown tha
43   <p>If you're out of allspice and
   an alternative.</p>
44 ▭ <p><img src="images/stylized_spi
45        <!-- End right column sectio
```

Wrap the selection in a `<div>` and
apply the ID **columnRight**

12 Select everything between content
section comments

The content section contains all of the code for
the right, center, and left column `<div>` tags.

Wrap it in a `<div>` and apply the
ID **content**

This "content" `<div>` formats the content of
the entire page, so that it's centered and
contained in an area that's 800 pixels wide,
regardless of the size of the browser window.

13 Switch to Design view

(Click to deselect the content, if necessary.) The
content sections are positioned according to the
CSS styles attached to the IDs you applied.

14 Save the page and preview it in
Internet Explorer

You'll continue to work on this page in the next
activity.

Close the browser

Modifying CSS rules

Explanation

Dreamweaver's CSS Rule Definition dialog box organizes CSS styles into several categories, as shown in Exhibit 1-5. Each category contains a set of style definitions.

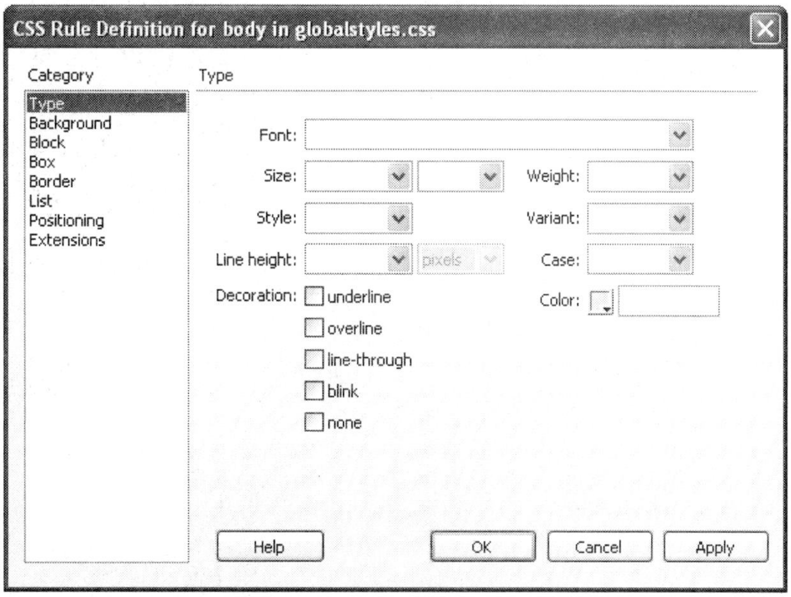

Exhibit 1-5: The CSS Rule Definition dialog box

To edit an existing CSS rule, double-click the rule in the CSS Styles panel. Then, edit the definitions in the CSS Rule Definition dialog box.

The box model

The *box model* is the layout model of CSS. Every rendered HTML element creates a box. The styles of the box model are those that directly influence the appearance of an element's box: its height, width, borders, padding, and margins.

For example, assume that the text "Element content" in Exhibit 1-6 is defined by a level-one heading (an <h1> tag). The solid line around the heading is its border, and the space between the content and the border is the element's padding. An element's margin is the space between its border and adjacent elements. You can control these and other styles by setting values in the Box category of the CSS Rule Definition dialog box.

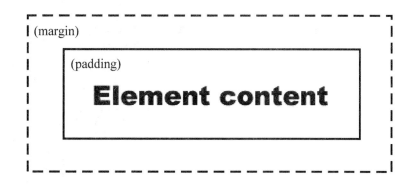

Exhibit 1-6: The box model

B-4: Editing CSS rules

Here's how	Here's why
1 In the CSS Styles panel, click **All**	(If necessary.) To display all CSS rules associated with the current document.
Expand globalstyles.css	
Double-click **body**	To open the CSS Rule Definition dialog box.
2 In the Category list, select **Background**	To view the style properties of the Background category.
3 Observe the Background image list	The background image is a JPEG, located in the images folder.
4 Observe the Repeat list	Nothing is selected, which means that, by default, the background image will repeat, or "tile," horizontally and vertically. You'll change this rule, so that the background image doesn't repeat.
From the Repeat list, select **no-repeat**	
Click **Apply**	To apply the change without closing the dialog box.
5 Observe the Attachment list	The fixed setting means that the image won't scroll with the rest of the page content.
Observe the Horizontal position and Vertical position lists	The image is fixed to the bottom-right corner of the browser window.
Click **OK**	To close the dialog box.
6 Preview the page in Internet Explorer	A dialog box appears, prompting you to save the changes you made to the external style sheet.
Click **Yes**	To close the dialog box and open the browser window.
Resize the browser window horizontally and vertically	The background image remains fixed in place regardless of the size of the browser window.
Scroll up and down	(If there are no scroll bars, resize the browser window, so that it's smaller.) To verify that the background image remains fixed in place.
7 Close the browser window	

8 Observe the right column in the layout	The top of the right column is flush with the bottom of the navigation bar. However, the other two columns have space above them. You'll modify the right column to align it with the other two columns.
9 In the CSS Styles panel, double-click **#columnRight**	(Scroll down if necessary.) You'll add a top margin to the rule to shift the box down, so that it aligns vertically with the other two columns.
10 In the Category list, select **Box**	To view the Box model styles, which include an element's height, width, padding, and margins.
Under Margin, in the Top box, enter **10**	
Verify that pixels is selected in the list to the right of the box	
Click **OK**	The right column now aligns with the other two columns.
11 Select the columnRight `<div>` by clicking its top edge, as shown	
Point anywhere in the selected content, as shown	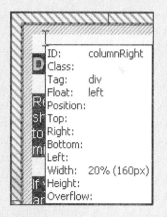
	A screen tip appears, showing the CSS properties associated with this `<div>` section.
12 Activate and save globalstyles.css	
	The style sheet opened automatically when you edited the first rule.
Switch to index.html	Next, you'll create a CSS rule to format the copyright section.

Selector types

Explanation

When you create a new CSS rule in Dreamweaver, you can select one of three selector types in the New CSS Rule dialog box. The three types are Class, Tag, and Advanced. Selectors select the element(s) on the page to which to apply the style properties.

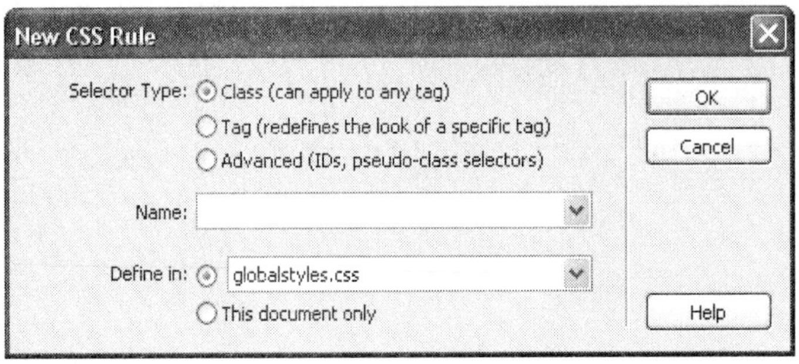

Exhibit 1-7: The New CSS Rule dialog box

Class selectors

With class selectors, you can apply a style rule to multiple different elements on a page. For example, if you want to create a specific kind, or class, of a paragraph, you can create a CSS rule using a class selector, with a name such as "notePara." You can then apply that class to as many paragraphs as needed. Only paragraphs that have been assigned that class name pick up the styles in that CSS rule. You could also use the class on any other element—it wouldn't be limited to paragraphs.

Tag selectors

Tag selectors apply styles to all instances of an HTML element. Browsers apply default styles to many HTML elements, so creating CSS rules with tag selectors allows you to redefine the styles for an element. For example, you can create a CSS rule that makes the text inside every `<h1>` tag blue.

Pseudo-class selectors

Pseudo-class selectors apply styles to links in their various states, such as the "hover" state and "visited" state.

ID selectors

ID styles must be unique; they can be applied only once per page. If the pages in your site have a consistent navigation bar, you should define that section with a `<div>` and an ID that logically names or describes the section, such as "navbar." Then, you apply a CSS rule to it by using an ID selector.

To create an ID style:

1   Open a style sheet or a Web page that's linked to a style sheet.

2   In the CSS Styles panel, click the New CSS Rule button.

3   In the New CSS Rule dialog box, under Selector type, select Advanced.

4   In the Selector box, enter an ID name for the rule. An ID must begin with the # sign.

5   Under Define in, do one of the following:

   • In the list, select a new or existing style sheet file.

   • Select This document only (to insert the rule in the current document).

6   Click OK.

7   In the CSS Rule Definition dialog box, specify the styles for the rule.

8   Click OK.

B-5: Creating and applying an ID style

Here's how	Here's why
1 In the CSS panel, click 🔲	(The New CSS Rule button.) To open the New CSS Rule dialog box.
Next to Selector Type, verify that **Advanced** is selected	
Edit the Selector box to read **#copyright**	To create an ID rule named copyright.
Next to Define in, verify that **globalstyles.css** is selected	You'll save this rule in the external style sheet.
Click **OK**	To open the CSS Rule Definition dialog box. The style name appears in the CSS panel.
2 In the Type category, in the Size box, enter **10**	To make the font size 10 pixels. (Pixels are the default unit of measurement.)
From the Style list, select **italic**	
3 In the Background category, click the Background color box	A color palette appears, and the pointer changes to an eyedropper.
Select the color #99CC33, as shown	
	To apply a green background color to the copyright section.
4 In the Block category, from the Text align list, select **center**	To center the text horizontally.
5 In the Box category, from the Clear list, select **both**	Applying the clear property to an element prevents another element from floating to one or both sides. In this case, selecting "both" causes the element to appear below the three columns, because they all have a float property applied to them.
6 Click **OK**	Even though you created the style, you need to apply it to the copyright text for it to take effect.
7 View the page in Code view	

8 In the copyright section, select the copyright text

```
51    <!-- Begin copyright section -->
52 ▣  Copyright Outlander Spices 2005-
53        <!-- End copyright section -
```

At the bottom of the page.

   Wrap it in a `<div>` and apply the copyright ID to it

Click the Insert Div Tag button, select copyright from the ID list, and click OK.

9 View the page in Design view

   Observe the copyright text

The copyright section is formatted with the styles you set for the copyright ID.

10 In the document toolbar, click

To display the Visual Aid list.

   From the list, select **CSS Layout Backgrounds**

To color code the `<div>` sections. The colors make it easier to identify sections in box layouts. These colors appear only in Dreamweaver.

11 Save the page and preview it in Internet Explorer

   Close the browser

12 Save and close all open files

Unit summary: CSS layout

Topic A   In this topic, you identified some of the advantages of **CSS layouts**. You learned how HTML and CSS work together to establish a page's design, and you identified the difference between **internal** and **external style sheets** and when you would use each.

Topic B   In this topic, you learned how to create and attach an external style sheet to a page. Then, you learned about the **<div> tag** and how you can use it to define content sections to establish a page layout, as well as to ensure consistency across multiple pages. Finally, you learned how to create and apply **ID styles** and modify CSS rules.

Independent practice activity

In this activity, you'll attach an external style sheet to a page. Then you'll define content sections with <div> tags and IDs. Finally, you'll modify a CSS rule and view the results.

1 Create a new site named **CSS practice**, using the Practice subfolder as your local root folder. (Make sure you start with the current unit folder.)

2 Open aboutus.html.

3 Attach the globalstyles.css style sheet to the page. (*Hint:* The style sheet is in the styles folder.)

4 Insert a new <div> container before the navigation bar text at the top of the page. Apply the existing "logo" ID to this <div> section, and delete the placeholder text. (*Hint:* Place the insertion point before the navigation bar text, then click the Insert Div Tag icon in the Insert bar.)

5 Switch to Code view.

6 In the masthead section, below the new "logo" <div> tags, wrap the navigation bar text links in a new <div> and give it the ID **globalNav**.

7 Create a new ID style in the globalstyles style sheet named **#fullpagecentered**. Navigate to the Box category, and then set the left and right margins at **20%**. Click **OK** to close the CSS Rule Definition dialog box.

8 Wrap all the content in the main content section in a new <div> and give it the ID **fullpagecentered**. (*Hint:* You'll have to scroll to select all the content.)

9 Wrap the content in the copyright section in a new <div> and give it the ID **copyright**.

10 Switch to Design view. The main content looks too narrow. You'll change the appropriate CSS style to make the column wider.

11 In the CSS Styles panel, double-click **#fullpagecentered**. In the Box category, change the left and right page margins to **15%** and click **OK**.

12 Preview the page in Internet Explorer. The finished results should look similar to the example in Exhibit 1-8.

13 Close the browser, and close all open files.

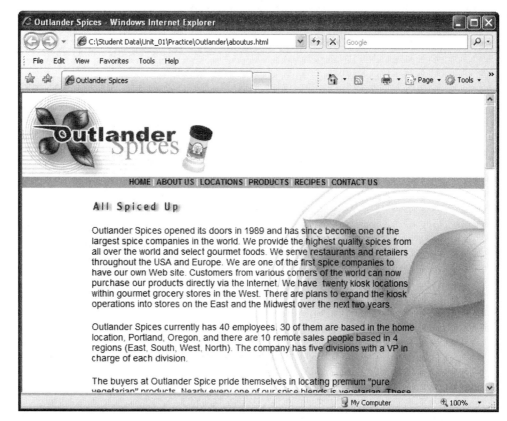

Exhibit 1-8: The completed aboutus.html page

Review questions

1 Structuring your documents in a meaningful, logical hierarchy of elements provides which benefits? (Choose all that apply.)

A It helps to establish consistency throughout a page or a site.

B It saves you time and effort when you later update a site.

C It allows your pages to be indexed by search engines more efficiently.

D It increases your site traffic.

E It allows Dreamweaver to function optimally.

2 You might want to place a CSS rule in an internal style sheet if:

A You want the rule to help establish consistency across multiple pages.

B You need the rule to apply to an element in that page only.

C You need the rule to apply to several individual pages, but not all the pages in a site.

D You want the rule to be ignored in Dreamweaver but applied in a browser.

3 If you want to apply a CSS rule to all instances of a particular HTML element, what selector type should you specify in the New CSS Rule dialog box?

   A Class

   B Tag

   C Advanced

   D ID

4 Which toolbar can you use to render your pages for various media types?

   A Document toolbar

   B Standard toolbar

   C Insert toolbar

   D Style Rendering toolbar.

5 What's the term used to describe pages that are divided into sections using <div> tags, and then formatted using styles?

   A Box model

   B Group layouts

   C Sectioning

   D Div layouts

6 If you want to define a unique section that holds the navigation bar, and you want this element to look the same on every page, it's best to:

   A Create an internal class style and give it a meaningful name, such as "navbar."

   B Create an external class style and give it a meaningful name, such as "navbar."

   C Create an internal ID style and give it a meaningful name, such as "navbar."

   D Create an external ID style and give it a meaningful name, such as "navbar."

7 You'd want to use an ID selector if:

   A You want to define the styles for a content section that appears only once in a page.

   B You want to define the styles for a content section that exists more than once in a page.

   C The element you're applying it to is a <div>.

   D The element you're applying it to is *not* a <div>.

Unit 2

Site assets

Unit time: 60 minutes

Complete this unit, and you'll know how to:

A Create, place, and update library items, and create and use snippets.

B Create, place, and edit server-side includes.

C Create a page template, define regions, and apply the template to other site pages.

D Create and edit head elements, and add keywords and a description to a page.

Topic A: Library assets

This topic covers the following Adobe ACE exam objectives for Dreamweaver CS3.

#	Objective
3.5	Create and use reusable page objects by using library items.
3.7	Create and use code Snippets.

Working with library assets

Explanation

A *library* is a special Dreamweaver file in which you can store assets for your Web pages. Such assets include images, tables, sound files, and video files. When you place an asset in a library, it's easy to use it multiple times in your site, as needed, and if you make a change to a library item, all instances of that item are updated automatically.

The Library panel, shown in Exhibit 2-1, makes it easy to re-use common elements. For example, if you want to insert an image in several pages in your site, you can place the image in a library and then drag it onto the desired pages from the library. If you make changes to the image in the library, all instances of the image are updated automatically. This can save you a lot of time and effort in the development process, when you're working with files that might not be finalized.

Exhibit 2-1: Library items in the Assets panel

Library items are stored in a library folder within the root folder of your site. The folder is created automatically when you add a library item. Each site has its own unique library.

Do it!   **A-1: Creating and inserting a library item**

Here's how	Here's why
1 Choose **Site**, **New Site...**	You'll create a new site in the current unit folder. You need to create a site before you can use the Assets panel.
Edit the Site name box to read **Outlander assets**	In the Advanced tab.
In the Local root folder box, open and select the Outlander folder	Click the folder icon, navigate to the current unit folder, open the Outlander folder, and click Select.
Click **OK**	To create the site. The site files appear in the Files panel.
2 Open index.html	(In the Files panel, double-click index.html.) You'll create a library item that you can reuse in multiple pages.
3 Activate the Assets panel	In the Files panel group.
Click 📖	(The Library button.) To activate the Library section of the Assets panel.
4 On the page, click the green spice shaker graphic, as shown	(The image is in the lower-right corner of index.html) To select it.
5 In the Assets panel, click ⊟	(The New Library Item button.) The graphic appears in the preview pane, and an untitled library item appears in the Library list.
6 Type **Spice shaker graphic** and press ← ENTER	To name the library item.

7	Activate the Files panel	A folder named Library is added to the Outlander folder. It contains the Spice shaker graphic.lbi file you created. You'll add the library item to another page.
8	Open recipes.html	From the Files panel.
9	Click to place the insertion point at the end of the recipe in the first column, as shown	alt. Cook for 5 minutes arm water. Bring to a ok until the potatoes is thick.|
	Press (↵ ENTER) twice	To insert a new paragraph.
10	Activate the Assets panel	
	Select the Spice shaker graphic library item	
	Click **Insert**	To add the image below the recipe.
11	Click another area of the page	(If necessary.) To deselect the graphic. The graphic is highlighted, indicating that it's a library item.
12	Preview the page in Internet Explorer	The highlighting appears only in Dreamweaver.
	Close the browser	

Updating a library item

Explanation

When you use a library item, the item itself isn't inserted in a page. Instead, Dreamweaver inserts a copy of the HTML code for that item into the page. It also includes an HTML comment that indicates a reference to the library item. Because each instance of a library item is a reference to the original library item, you can update all instances simply by updating the original library item.

To update a library item:

1. In the Library panel, select the item you want to update, and click Edit. The item opens in a separate document window.
2. Edit the item in the document window, and save the file.
3. In the Update Library Items dialog box, click Update. The Update Pages dialog box appears.
4. Click Close.

Detach library items

If you need to edit an instance of a library item, but you don't want to change the original library item, you can detach it. By doing so, you sever the link, allowing you to edit the item independently of the original. This process also prevents the page item from being updated if the original library item is changed. To detach a library item, you can select the instance you want to detach and, in the Property inspector, click Detach from original. In addition, you could right-click the instance you want to detach and choose Detach From Original.

Do it!

A-2: Updating a library item

Here's how	Here's why
1 In the Assets panel, select **Spice shaker graphic**	You'll swap the current image with another image of a spice shaker.
Click	(The Edit button.) To open Spice shaker graphic.lbi.
2 Delete the spice shaker graphic from the page	
3 Activate the Files panel	
Expand the images subfolder	
4 Drag spice_bottle.gif to the page	The Image Tag Accessibility Attributes dialog box appears.
In the Alternate text box, type **Spice shaker graphic**	
Click **OK**	To add the image to the page.
5 Save Spice shaker graphic.lib	The Update Library Items dialog box opens.
Click **Update**	To open the Update Pages dialog box.
Click **Close**	To close the dialog box.
Close Spice shaker graphic.lbi	To return to the Recipes page. The page now uses the new graphic.
6 Switch to index.html	To view the updated library item.

Snippets

Another way that you can add repeating elements to your pages is by using the Snippets panel, shown in Exhibit 2-2. *Snippets* are sections of code that you can store and retrieve whenever you need them. Even if you're experienced with HTML, there are other languages, such as JavaScript or ActionScript, which you might need to draw on as you work on a site. Using the Snippets panel can save you time, because you can store frequently used code blocks and scripts and then add them, as needed, instead of typing the code by hand each time or having to reference an external file for copy and paste purposes.

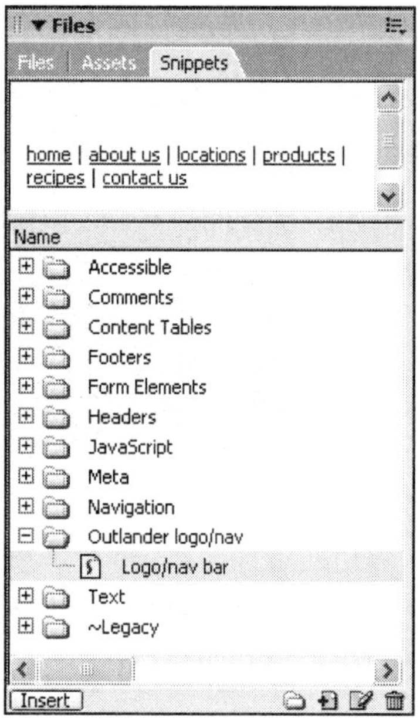

Exhibit 2-2: The Snippets panel

To create a snippet, select the code you want to use for the snippet, then click the New Snippet button at the bottom of the Snippets panel. A dialog box appears in which you can name the snippet, add a description, and select options to control how you want to add the snippet to other site pages.

To add a snippet to a page, place the insertion point where you want the snippet, then double-click the snippet in the Snippets panel. You can add snippets in both Design view and Code view.

Do it!   **A-3:   Creating and inserting a snippet**

Here's how	Here's why
1 Switch to Code view	(In index.html.) You'll create and use a code snippet.
2 Activate the Snippets panel	In the Files panel group.
Click	The New Snippets Folder button is at the bottom of the Snippets panel.
Name the new folder **Outlander logo/nav**	
3 Select the masthead section, as shown	
4 Click	(The New Snippet button is at the bottom of the Snippets panel.) To open the Snippet dialog box.
In the Name box, enter **Logo/Nav bar**	To name the snippet.
In the Description box, enter **Outlander logo and navigation bar**	
5 Verify that **Wrap selection** is selected	
Beside Preview type, select **Design**	To show the logo and nav bar in the snippet preview, instead of its code.
Click **OK**	To close the dialog box and add the snippet.
Observe the Snippets panel	It should look like the one illustrated in Exhibit 2-2.
6 Create a new, blank page	
Save the page as **gallery.html**	In the Outlander folder, in the current unit folder.
Insert a line within the body section, as shown	

7	Double-click Logo/nav bar	(In the Snippets panel.) The code snippet is added to the page.
	Click in Design view	To update the page. The logo doesn't appear, and the navigation bar isn't formatted, because the page isn't yet linked to a style sheet.
8	Activate the CSS Styles panel	If necessary.
9	Click [icon]	(The Attach Style Sheet button.) To open the Attach External Style Sheet dialog box.
	Click **Browse**	The Select Style Sheet File dialog box appears.
	Navigate to the Styles folder	In the Outlander folder.
	Select **globalstyles.css** and click **OK**	To select the style sheet and return to the Attach External Style Sheet dialog box.
10	Verify that **Link** is selected	
	Click **OK**	To close the dialog box and attach the style sheet.
11	Observe the page in Design view	The logo and background image appear, and the navigation bar is formatted.
12	Save and close gallery.html	

Topic B: Server-side includes

This topic covers the following Adobe ACE exam objective for Dreamweaver CS3.

#	Objective
3.6	Explain the purpose of and how to use server-side includes.

Using server-side includes

Server-side includes are similar to library items, except that they're maintained by the server after you upload your site. They provide an efficient way to update pages without having to make the changes manually and then re-upload them. For example, some sites might need to make frequent changes to certain types of information, such as copyright statements, event listings, or news items. Using server-side includes, you can upload one file (the server-side include), and the server automatically replaces the content in pages that reference it.

In general, server-side includes are a good way to update site pages when:

- Your site requires frequent editing.
- Your site is large.
- Two or more people manage the site from different locations.
- A client is updating the site and doesn't have Dreamweaver to take advantage of library items. (However, clients would be required to understand how to update the content themselves in the SSI document and how to upload the document to the server.)

Before you incorporate server-side includes in your site, you should check with your service provider to ensure that they support them and to find out what naming conventions are required. Some servers are configured to examine all files to see if they have server-side includes, whereas other servers search only for files with the .shtml (or .shtm) extension.

To create a server-side include:

1 Open the document that contains the content you want to use for the server-side include.
2 In Design view, select the content you want to include.
3 Switch to Code view, then choose Edit, Copy.
4 Create a new blank HTML document.
5 In Code view, select all the existing code, then press Delete.
6 Choose Edit, Paste to paste the server-side include content.
7 Save the file as an HTML document. (If your service provider requires the .shtml or .shtm extension, name your file with that extension instead.)

Do it!   **B-1:   Creating a server-side include**

Here's how	Here's why
1 In the index document, in Design view, scroll down to view the copyright statement	(If necessary.) The copyright statement appears on every page. You'll create a server-side include to make updating the copyright statement easier, should it be necessary after the site is uploaded to a server.
2 Click anywhere in the copyright statement	To place the insertion point.
In the tag selector, click **<div#copyright>**	
	To select the entire copyright box.
3 Switch to Code view	The opening and closing <div> tags surrounding the copyright statement are selected.
Press CTRL + C	To copy the code.
4 Create a new, blank HTML document	Because you were in Code view previously, the new document is in Code view, as well.
5 Press CTRL + A	To select all the default page code.
Press DELETE	To delete the code.
6 Press CTRL + V	To paste the copyright code.
	`1    <div id="copyright">Content for`
7 Save the document as **copyright.shtml**	This document contains the content for the server-side include. (The formatting for the copyright statement is included in the globalstyles style sheet.)
8 Close the document	

Inserting server-side includes

Explanation

After you've created a server-side include, you can reference it in any of the site pages. When the server parses the site pages, that is, when a user references them in a browser, the server searches for the server-side include document and inserts its contents into the page.

To place a server-side include in a page:

1 Open the page in which you want to add the server-side include.

2 In Design view, place the cursor where you want to add the server-side include.

3 In the Common category in the Insert bar, click the Server-Side Include button. (You can also choose Insert, Server-Side Include.) The Select File dialog box appears.

4 Navigate to and select the server-side include document.

5 Click OK.

Although you can preview server-side includes in your Dreamweaver pages, they aren't visible if you preview your pages locally in a browser. In order for them to work, they need to reside on your server.

Do it!

B-2: Adding a server-side include

Here's how	Here's why
1 In the index document, switch to Split view	The copyright box is still selected.
2 Press (DELETE)	To remove the copyright statement. In Code view, the insertion point is visible just after the "Begin copyright section" comment tag. This is where you'll insert the server-side include.
3 Select the Common category in the Insert bar	If necessary.
4 In the Insert bar, click 🗋	(The Server-Side Include button.) The Select File dialog box appears.
In the Outlander folder, select **copyright.shtml** and click **OK**	This is the server-side include you created earlier.
5 In Design view, scroll down to view the copyright statement	If necessary.

6 Click the copyright text	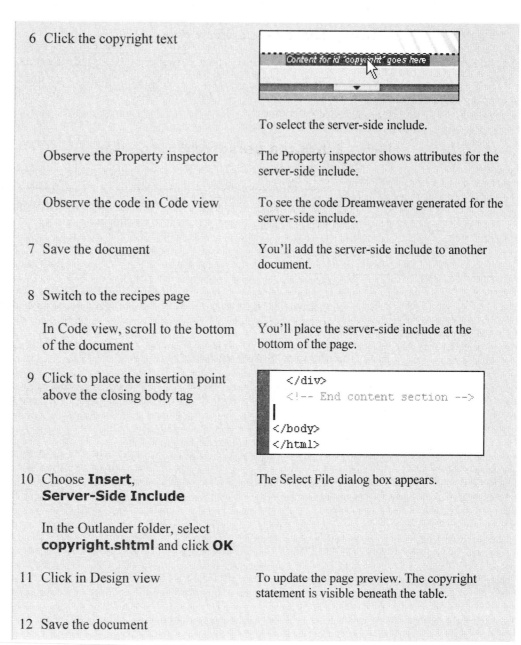
	To select the server-side include.
Observe the Property inspector	The Property inspector shows attributes for the server-side include.
Observe the code in Code view	To see the code Dreamweaver generated for the server-side include.
7 Save the document	You'll add the server-side include to another document.
8 Switch to the recipes page	
In Code view, scroll to the bottom of the document	You'll place the server-side include at the bottom of the page.
9 Click to place the insertion point above the closing body tag	
10 Choose **Insert**, **Server-Side Include**	The Select File dialog box appears.
In the Outlander folder, select **copyright.shtml** and click **OK**	
11 Click in Design view	To update the page preview. The copyright statement is visible beneath the table.
12 Save the document	

In the code image:

```
    </div>
    <!-- End content section -->

</body>
</html>
```

Editing server-side includes

Explanation

To edit a server-side include, open the server-side include document, make the necessary changes, and then save it. When you upload (or re-upload) the server-side include document to the server, the changes are automatically visible throughout the site on pages that reference it.

Do it!

B-3:   Editing a server-side include

Here's how	Here's why
1 In the recipes page, double-click the copyright statement	To open the copyright.shtml document.
2 In Design view, triple-click the copyright text	To select it.
Type **Contents © Outlander Spices**	The © code is the character entity for the copyright symbol.
3 Save and close the document	
4 Observe the copyright statement in the recipes page	The text is changed to what you specified in the server-side include document.
5 Switch to the index page using Design view	The copyright statement is updated universally. If the site were uploaded to a server, you'd only need to re-upload the server-side include document for the changes to be made throughout the site.
6 Save and close all open documents	

Topic C: Page templates

This topic covers the following Adobe ACE exam objective for Dreamweaver CS3.

#	Objective
2.8	Explain how templates are used to architect for reuse and consistency.

Working with templates

Explanation

If you have multiple pages that share a common layout and common elements, a template can help you develop those pages faster and more efficiently. With a template, you can design a layout that contains fixed page elements, and you can specify areas of a page that can be edited. You can then apply that template to multiple pages, changing the content in the editable areas while maintaining the content in the fixed areas.

Templates can be especially useful if you're working with a team of people to develop a site. For example, one developer might create the overall design, with editable regions designated for content unique to each page. Other developers could then be responsible for adding page-specific content but wouldn't be able to modify the fixed regions established by the designer.

Templates can also help you maintain consistency across your site pages and make site maintenance faster and easier. If changes to fixed areas of a template need to be made, changing them in the template applies the changes to all pages that are based on the template.

To create a template from a page:

1 Create or open the page that you want to convert to a template.
2 Choose File, Save as Template. The Save as Template dialog box appears.
3 From the Site list, select the site you want to save the template into. In the Save as box, enter a unique name for the template and click Save.

Editable regions

Every template needs to contain at least one editable region for page-specific content.

To create an editable region in a template:

1 Select the content that you want to set as an editable region or place the insertion point where you want to create the editable region.
2 Choose Insert, Template Objects, Editable Region. The Editable Region dialog box appears.
3 In the Name box, enter a unique name for the editable region and click OK.

Repeating and Optional regions

Sometimes you might want to repeat a template section in a page, or you might want to include content that is only visible on certain pages. You can do this using Repeating and Optional regions in your template pages.

Repeating regions provide a way to repeat certain portions of content in your pages. For example, you might use a template that includes a table, but you're unsure of how many table rows you need on each page. With repeating regions you can create and format the first table row and then repeat the content as many times as necessary.

(handwritten margin notes: "If Forget to Update pages" and "Modify a Template" and "f5")

The template user uses repeat region control options to add or delete copies of the repeated region in the document.

Optional regions provide a way to include content that you might not need on every page. For example, you can create an optional region for a Back To Top link that can be either visible or hidden, depending on the length of the text on the page. Both Repeating and Optional regions can be editable or non-editable.

To create Repeating and Optional regions in a template, choose either Optional Region or Repeating Region from the Template Objects submenu, then enter a name and set any region attributes, if applicable, in the corresponding dialog box.

The tag selector

Sometimes it can be difficult to select objects in Design view. For example, sometimes you might want to select multiple elements that are within a set of tags, such as the entire contents of a `<div>` container. To ensure that you're selecting everything you want, you can use the tag selector in the status bar, as shown in Exhibit 2-3. To make a selection, place the insertion point on the page within the object(s) you want to select. In the tag selector, click to select the tag surrounding the objects.

Exhibit 2-3: Making a selection using the tag selector

Do it!

C-1: Creating a template

Here's how	Here's why
1 Open aboutus.html	You'll create a page template from an existing Web page.
2 Choose **File, Save as Template...**	To open the Save As Template dialog box.
Edit the Save as box to read **fullpage**	
In the Description box, enter **Basic full page layout**	To add a description to the template.
Click **Save**	A dialog box appears, asking if you'd like to update links.
3 Click **Yes**	The file is saved as a DWT (Dreamweaver Template) file.

4 In the Files panel, expand the Templates folder

To view the template document.

5 In the template, place the insertion point in the main content

(The area with the paragraphs.) You'll delete this section and replace it with an editable region.

Press CTRL + A

To select everything in the `<div>` tag.

Type **Page content**

This will serve as placeholder text for the editable region.

6 Triple-click **Page content**

To select the text. You want the text, not the container it resides in, to be editable.

7 Choose **Insert**, **Template Objects**, **Editable Region**

The New Editable Region dialog box opens.

Edit the Name box to read **MainContent**

Click **OK**

The area is marked as an editable region.

8 Click to place the insertion point in the "Go to top" text	(In the lower-left corner.) Because this link is necessary only for pages with large amounts of content, you'll make it an Optional region.
In the tag selector, click **<div#topofpage>**	
	Because this is an optional region, you want the entire container to be part of the region.
9 Choose **Insert**, **Template Objects**, **Optional Region**	The New Optional Region dialog box opens.
Edit the Name box to read **TopPage**	
Click **OK**	Some pages will also not require the sub navigation bar.
10 Select the box containing the sub navigation bar	
	Click to place the insertion point in the sub navigation bar, then in the tag selector, click <div#subNav>.
11 Choose **Insert**, **Template Objects**, **Optional Region**	The New Optional Region dialog box opens.
Edit the Name box to read **SubNav**	
Click **OK**	
12 Save and close the template	You'll continue to work with this template in the next activity.

Creating a page from a template

Explanation   You can create a new page from a template, or you can apply a template to an existing page. When you apply a template to a page that has existing content, you need to assign the content to the template's editable regions. However, when you create a new page with no existing content other than the fixed content of the template, there's no need to match that content to the template's editable regions.

To create a new page from a template:

1   Choose File, New. The New Document dialog box opens.
2   From the list on the left, select Page from Template.
3   From the Site list, select the site that includes the template.
4   From the Template list, select the template you want to use for the new page.
5   Click Create to create a new, untitled document based on the template.

Modifying template properties

Sometimes you might need to modify an editable tag attribute from within a template-based document. For example, if the template includes an Optional region, you might want to show or hide the optional content.

To modify template properties:

1 Open the template-based document.

2 Choose Modify, Template Properties to open the Template Properties dialog box, shown in Exhibit 2-4.

3 In the Name column, select the attribute you want to change, then select from the available options.

4 Click OK.

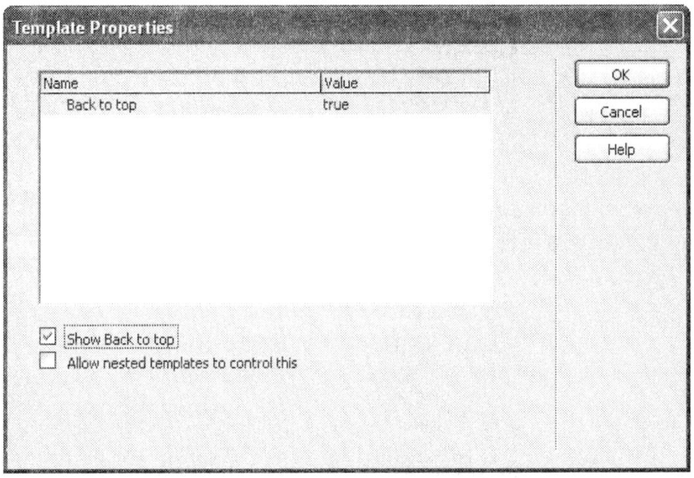

Exhibit 2-4: The Template Properties dialog box

Applying a template

You can apply a template to an existing page. If the page hasn't had a template applied to it before, Dreamweaver displays the Inconsistent Region Names dialog box, shown in Exhibit 2-5, so that you can match the existing content with the template's editable region(s).

To apply a template to an existing page:

1 Open the page to which you want to apply the template.

2 In the Assets panel, click the Templates button.

3 In the Templates list, drag the template to the document window. The Inconsistent Region Names dialog box appears.

4 In the document, select the content you want to apply to a region.

5 From the Move content to new region list, select the region you want to use for the selected content.

6 Repeat steps 4 and 5 for the remaining page content.

7 Click OK.

Inconsistent Region Names   ☒

Some regions in this document have no corresponding regions in the new template.

Name	Resolved
⊟ Editable regions	
┌──Document body	<Not resolved>
└──Document head	<Not resolved>

Move content to new region: [   ] ▾ [Use for all]

[Help]   [Cancel] [OK]

Exhibit 2-5: The Inconsistent Region Names dialog box

Template expressions

A template expression is a variable or parameter in the template that allows you to use a template in various ways. For example, you can use template expressions to show or hide certain optional areas in the template, depending on a condition that you establish, or you can use them to set up a template that automatically numbers table rows and embedded table rows to create an auto-numbering outline. Template expressions require hand-coding and a general understanding of the expression language Dreamweaver uses for templates, which is based on JavaScript.

Do it!

C-2: Applying a page template

Here's how	Here's why
1 Choose **File, New...**	You'll create a new Web page based on the template you created.
2 On the left side of the dialog box, select **Page from Template**	
In the Site list, select **Outlander assets**	(If necessary.) The template "fullpage" appears in the Template for list.
Observe the Description box	A thumbnail of the page and the description you entered earlier appear.
3 Select **fullpage**	
4 Verify that **Update page when template changes** is checked	
Click **Create**	To create a new, untitled page based on this template.

5 Save the page as **books.html**

6 Point to an empty area of the page

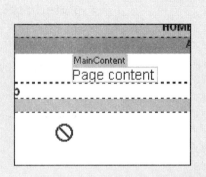

The pointer changes to indicate that you can't edit this area of the page. Only areas designated as editable regions can be modified.

7 Drag **Books.doc** to the right of the "Page content" text, as shown

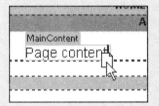

(Drag the file from the Files panel.) The Insert Document dialog box appears.

8 Verify that **Text with structure plus basic formatting** is selected

Verify that **Clean up Word paragraph spacing** is checked

Click **OK**

9 Delete the "Page content" text

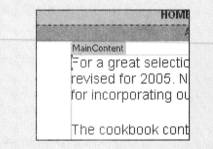

You don't need the sub navigation bar for this page. Also, because there isn't much content, you don't need the "Go to top" link.

10	Choose **Modify**, **Template Properties...**	To open the Template Properties dialog box.
	Clear **Show SubNav**	
11	In the Name column, click **TopPage**	To select the Optional region.
	Clear **Show TopPage**	
12	Click **OK**	Both the sub navigation bar and the "Go to top" link are hidden.
13	Save and close the document	You'll now apply the template to an existing page.
14	Open products.html	(From the Files panel.) This page contains an existing table with spice descriptions.
15	Activate the Assets panel	
16	Click [image]	The Templates button.
17	Click [image]	(The Refresh Site List button.) The template appears in the list.
	From the Templates list, drag **fullpage** to the page	The Inconsistent Region Names dialog box appears.
18	Select **Document body**	
	From the Move content to new region list, select **MainContent**	To move the existing content to that region in the template.
	Select **Document head**	
	From the Move content to new region list, select **head**	To move the existing content to the head region in the template.
	Click **OK**	The template is successfully applied to the page.
19	Hide the SubNav Optional region	Choose Modify, Template Properties, then clear the Show SubNav checkbox and click OK.
20	Save and close the document	

Topic D: Head elements

Explanation

The head section of a Web page contains resources for and information about the current document, such as a page title, keywords, CSS style rules or a link to a style sheet, and scripts. The contents of the head section don't appear in a browser.

Working with head elements

You can enter code directly in Code view. You can also create and manipulate several tags in the head section by entering values in the Property inspector and other areas of the Dreamweaver interface. The following table describes common head elements.

Item	Description
Meta tags	*Meta tags* include keywords that are relevant to the page's content and which are used by some search engines to help users locate information, and a description, which is used by some search engines to categorize and summarize your site. Meta tags also specify page properties, such as character encoding, the author, or copyright information.
Title	The *title tag* holds the text that displays in the browser's title bar. Search engines refer to a Web page by its title.
JavaScript	The head section typically holds any *JavaScript* code, or links to external scripts.
Reference links	The head section can include a link to files, such as external style sheets.
Style	The style section holds the CSS styles that comprise a page's internal style sheet.
Page properties	Page properties might include text colors or a background image for the page. (However, it's best to use a style sheet to establish text colors and background images.)

Site description and keywords

A site's description and keywords can be important to the site's effectiveness with search engines. When a user submits search terms, search engines return a list of sites, usually listed according to the best match. Writing effective keywords and a page or site description can help improve your ranking in some search engines.

Descriptions can improve the overall quality of the search result. For example, Google and Yahoo use a site's description as the text that appears below a Web site's link in many search results. If a description isn't present, some search engines use the first text it encounters on the page, which might not be the presentation you're looking for.

Because you typically want visitors who your site to enter through the home page, it's often best to enter a description and list of keywords in the index (home) page. However, you can list keywords and descriptions for as many pages as you wish.

Do it!   **D-1: Discussing head elements**

Here's how	Here's why
1 Which elements might you want to include in the head section of your home page?	
2 What are some benefits of using meta tags?	
3 How can keyword meta tags help create more traffic to your site?	
4 Which Web pages in your site should be given keyword tags?	

Meta tag icons

Explanation

There are over 30 types of meta tags. Dreamweaver can display a list of head elements as icons in the document window, as shown in Exhibit 2-6. When you click a head element icon, its attributes appear in the Property inspector. To display a page's head content as a series of icons, choose View, Head Content. You can also select Head Content from the View options list in the Document toolbar or press Ctrl+Shift+H.

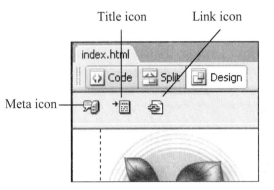

Exhibit 2-6: Head elements displayed as icons in the document window

Do it!

D-2: Examining a document's head section

Here's how	Here's why
1 Open index.html	You'll examine the elements in the head section.
2 Choose **View, Head Content**	To display the head section icons at the top of the document window.
3 Click [meta icon]	(The Meta icon.) To display the meta data in the document.
Observe the Property inspector	This page uses the ISO-8859-1 character set encoding, which is the best character set to use for languages that use a Latin alphabet, such as English. Dreamweaver writes this tag into the page by default.
4 Click [title icon]	(The Title icon.) To view the page title.
Observe the Property inspector	The title of this Web page is "Outlander Spices."
5 Click [link icon]	(The Link icon.) To display the style sheet linked to this page.
Observe the Property inspector	This page is linked to a style sheet named globalstyle.css.

Edit a head element

Explanation

Dreamweaver makes it easy to edit the content in your meta tags. Click the icon for the head element you want to edit, and then make the desired content changes in the Property inspector. Exhibit 2-7 shows the Property inspector when the title icon is selected.

Exhibit 2-7: Tag attributes in the Property inspector

Do it!

D-3: Editing a head element

Here's how	Here's why
1 Click the Title icon	You'll change the page title.
2 In the Property inspector, edit the Title box to read **Outlander Spices: Welcome!**	
3 View the page in Code view	The title tag and the new title are highlighted.
Return to Design view	
4 Preview the page in Internet Explorer	
Verify that the new title appears in the browser's title bar	
Close the browser	

Keywords

Explanation

Some search engines use meta keywords and descriptions to help provide accurate search results.

To enter keywords:

1 Scan your pages and create a list of words that are relevant to your site's purpose and content. Include words that might not appear in your site's content but that are likely to be entered by a user. For example, the word *seasonings* doesn't appear in the Outlander Spices Web site, but it could appear in a user's search.
2 Choose Insert, HTML, Head Tags, Keywords.
3 In the Keywords dialog box, type a list of keywords, separated by commas.
4 Click OK.

Do it!

D-4: Defining keywords for your site

Here's how	Here's why
1 Choose **Insert**, **HTML**, **Head Tags**, **Keywords**	To open the Keywords dialog box.
2 In the Keywords box, enter **spices**, **outlander**, **cooking**, **seasonings**, **ingredients**	To create a list of relevant keywords that users are likely to enter in a search engine.
Click **OK**	To add the keywords.
3 Observe the head section of the Document window	The Keywords icon appears.
4 Click the Keywords icon	
Observe the Property inspector	The keywords appear in the Keywords box.
5 Save index.html	

Descriptions

Explanation

Your site description should be a concise, summarizing statement that describes the purpose or content of your site. Most search engine users are looking for the best results as quickly as possible. Users are likely to skip over a long or poorly written description. Also, the search engine might display only the first line or two of the description.

To insert a description, choose Insert, HTML, Head Tags, Description. Enter your description in the Description dialog box, and click OK.

Do it!

D-5: Creating a description of your site

Here's how	Here's why
1 Choose **Insert**, **HTML**, **Head Tags**, **Description**	To open the Description dialog box. You'll add a description that a search engine might use to index your site and display on a search result page.
2 In the Description box, enter **Outlander Spices is the market leader in quality spices for cooking and baking of all kinds.** Click **OK**	
3 Observe the head section of the Document window	 The Description icon appears
4 Observe the Property inspector	The description appears in the Description box.
5 View the page in Code view Return to Design view	The meta tag you created is highlighted. The name of the tag is "Description," and the tag content is the actual description text.
6 Why is it important to write a concise, summarizing statement as your site description?	
7 Save and close index.html	

Unit summary: Site assets

Topic A In this topic, you learned how to create a **library item** and add it to a page. Then you learned how to edit and update a library item. You learned that you can update multiple pages by making changes to a library item. Finally, you learned how to create and use code **snippets**.

Topic B In this topic, you learned how to create a **server-side include** document, and reference it in site pages. You also learned how to update a server-side include. so that the changes are visible in all site pages that reference it.

Topic C In this topic, you learned how to create a **template** from an existing page. You defined **editable** and **optional regions**, and you created a new page based on the template.

Topic D In this unit, you learned about common **head elements** and explored the head section of a page. You also edited an existing head element, and finally, you learned how to add **keywords** and a **site description**.

Independent practice activity

In this activity, you'll create a new library item and add it to a page. Then you'll save the page as a template, add keywords and a description to the page, and create a new page from the template.

1 Create a new site named **Assets practice**, using the Outlander folder inside the Practice folder as the local root folder. (The Practice folder is located in the current unit folder.)

2 Open recipes.html.

3 Create a new library item named **recipeDisclaimer** that includes the following text: **When trying any new recipe, sample the results periodically and adjust the amount of spice to taste.** Make the text bold and italic. (*Hint*: Use the Assets panel to create a new library item.)

4 Add this new library item to recipes.html. Place it between the recipe and the copyright statement, as shown in Exhibit 2-8. (*Hint*: Drag the library item to the `<div>` tag above the copyright section.)

5 Save recipes.html as a template named **recipes**.

6 In the recipes template, make both columns editable regions. Then save and close the template.

7 Create a new page from the recipes.dwt template. Save the page as **turmeric.html**.

8 Delete the contents of the editable regions.

9 Save and close all open pages.

10 Open index.html.

11 View the document's head content.

12 Add the following keywords: **recipes**, **spices**, **outlander**.

13 Add a fitting description for the page.

14 Save and close index.html.

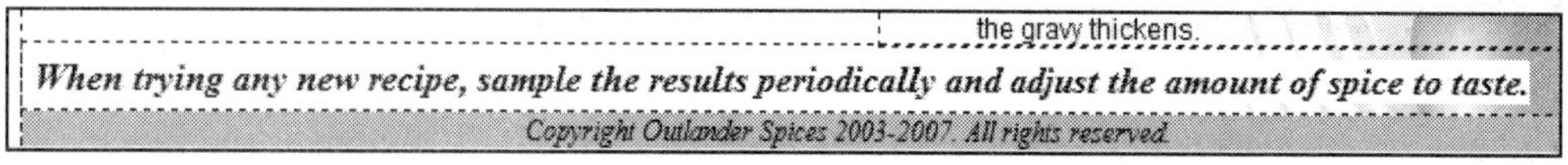

When trying any new recipe, sample the results periodically and adjust the amount of spice to taste.

Exhibit 2-8: The recipe.html page after step 4

Review questions

1 If you detach an instance of a library item and then edit the content on the page, the original library item:

   A Is deleted.

   B Is updated accordingly.

   C Isn't affected.

   D Replaces the changed content the next time the page is opened.

2 If your site consists of hundreds of pages, and each one of them contains the same library item for a page footer, what happens if you edit the original library item?

   A When you open each page in Dreamweaver, a dialog box asks if you want the item to be updated.

   B All instances of the item are updated automatically.

   C Only the open document is updated.

   D You can't edit the original library item.

3 What are small sections of code that you store and retrieve called?

   A Library items

   B Assets

   C Templates

   D Snippets

4 How can you place a server-side include in a page? (Choose all that apply.)

   A Place the insertion point where you want the server-side include, then choose Insert, Server-Side Include.

   B Place the insertion point where you want the server-side include, then drag from the Link pickwhip in the Property inspector to the server-side include file in the Files panel.

   C Place the insertion point where you want the server-side include, then click the Server-Side Include button in the Insert bar.

   D Right-click where you want the server-side include, then choose Add Server-Side Include.

5 If you apply a template to a page with existing content that wasn't designed for that template, what happens?

   A You can't apply a template to a page that wasn't created for that template.

   B Dreamweaver applies the template automatically.

   C Dreamweaver prompts you to specify which regions of the page content should apply to the template regions.

   D Dreamweaver prompts you to save the page as a new template file.

6 Which template region provides a way to include content that you might not need on every page?

   A Editable

   B Optional

   C Repeating

   D Temporary

7 How can you hide an optional template region in a page with a template applied?

   A Choose Modify, Template Properties. In the Name column, select the optional region you want to hide, then clear the Show checkbox.

   B Right-click the optional region content on the page, and choose Hide.

   C Open the template document, then right-click the optional region and choose Hide Region.

   D Triple-click the optional region content. In the Name column, select the optional region you want to hide, then clear the Show checkbox.

8 How can you display a page's head content in Design view? (Choose all that apply.)

   A Triple-click anywhere in the Document toolbar.

   B Choose View, Head Content.

   C Select Head Content from the View options list in the Document toolbar.

   D In the Property inspector, click Page Properties.

Unit 3
Forms

Unit time: 60 minutes

Complete this unit, and you'll know how to:

A Create an interactive form and add input components to it.

B Set the tab order of form fields.

Topic A: Form objects

Explanation

Web forms enable users to interact with your Web site. Typically, users fill out Web forms to create an account, make a purchase, or request information. The information entered on the form is often sent to a database. Dreamweaver makes it easy to create a form and add a variety of input components to it, as shown in Exhibit 3-1.

Building a form

In HTML, the `<form>` tag opens a form container. All the form code is contained inside the `<form>` tag. When a user clicks the form's Submit button, the input fields within the form are processed and sent to a Web server.

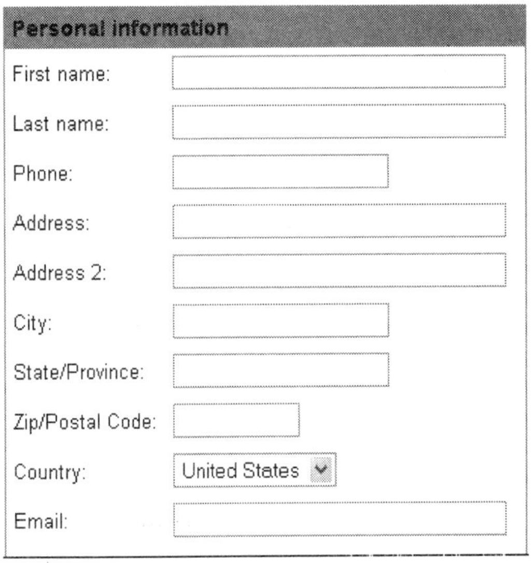
Personal information
First name:
Last name:
Phone:
Address:
Address 2:
City:
State/Province:
Zip/Postal Code:
Country:
United States
Email:

Exhibit 3-1: An example of a Web form

To start a form, place the insertion point where you want the form to appear, and then click the Form button on the Insert bar. You can also drag the Form button to the desired position on the page.

By default, form elements, such as text input fields, might not align neatly on a page. You can use a table inside the form to hold the form elements and keep them aligned for a more professional appearance. For example, the form shown in Exhibit 3-1 uses a table to align the form input fields.

Form objects

The Forms tab on the Insert bar displays an icon for each form object, as shown in Exhibit 3-2.

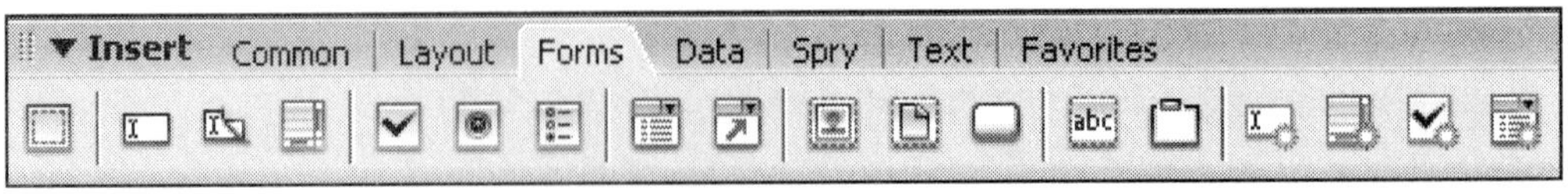
Insert
Common
Layout
Forms
Data
Spry
Text
Favorites

Exhibit 3-2: The Forms tab on the Insert bar

The following table describes some of the most commonly used form object icons.

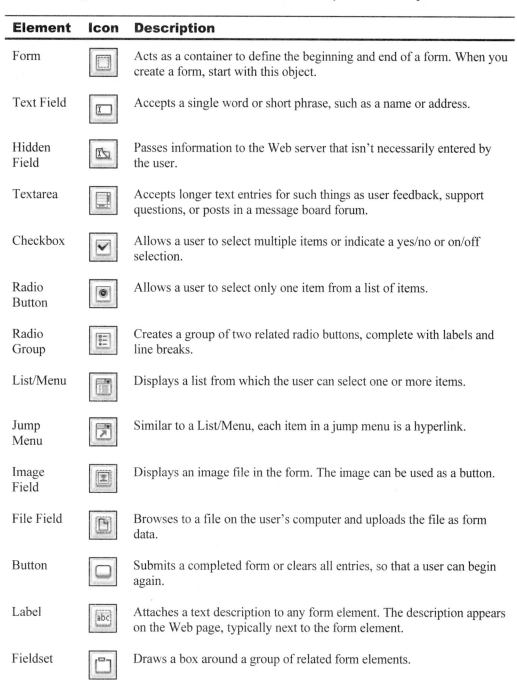

Element	Icon	Description
Form		Acts as a container to define the beginning and end of a form. When you create a form, start with this object.
Text Field		Accepts a single word or short phrase, such as a name or address.
Hidden Field		Passes information to the Web server that isn't necessarily entered by the user.
Textarea		Accepts longer text entries for such things as user feedback, support questions, or posts in a message board forum.
Checkbox		Allows a user to select multiple items or indicate a yes/no or on/off selection.
Radio Button		Allows a user to select only one item from a list of items.
Radio Group		Creates a group of two related radio buttons, complete with labels and line breaks.
List/Menu		Displays a list from which the user can select one or more items.
Jump Menu		Similar to a List/Menu, each item in a jump menu is a hyperlink.
Image Field		Displays an image file in the form. The image can be used as a button.
File Field		Browses to a file on the user's computer and uploads the file as form data.
Button		Submits a completed form or clears all entries, so that a user can begin again.
Label		Attaches a text description to any form element. The description appears on the Web page, typically next to the form element.
Fieldset		Draws a box around a group of related form elements.

Do it! **A-1: Creating a form**

Here's how	Here's why
1 Choose **Site**, **New Site...**	You'll define a new site.
Edit the Site name box to read **Outlander forms**	In the Advanced tab.
In the Local root folder box, navigate to the Outlander folder	Click the folder icon. Navigate to the current unit folder, open the Outlander folder, and click Select.
Click **OK**	To create the site. Dreamweaver displays the site in the Files panel.
2 Open inforequest.html	The page includes the basic structure you want for a form, including tables and text. You'll convert the content to a form, and add interactive form elements.
3 Place the insertion point as shown	
	You'll insert a form after this text.
4 Activate the Forms tab on the Insert bar	
Click [ ]	(The Form button.) To insert a new form at the insertion point.
5 Switch to Split view	

```
<!-- Begin main form section -->
  <div id="formMain">
    <h1>Request for information</h1>
    <form id="form1" name="form1" method="post" action="">
    </form>
</div>
```

	(To view the tags that Dreamweaver inserted.) Notice that the closing form tag is inserted directly after the opening tag. You need to be sure that all your form elements are inside this form container.
Switch to Design view	

6 Press ⏎ ENTER

You'll cut the two tables containing the text for the forms and paste them here.

7 Click as shown

To select the "formLeft" div section.

Press CTRL + X

To cut the section. You'll paste it inside the form container.

Place the insertion point as shown

Press CTRL + V

8 Cut the formRight div

Select it and press Ctrl+X.

Place the insertion point as shown

(To the right of the left column.) You'll paste the right div section here.

Paste the div

9 Save the page

Text fields and textarea fields

Explanation

A text field is meant for short, alphanumeric entries, usually a single line of text for such things as a name or address. A textarea field is meant for longer entries that may span multiple lines.

Textarea fields

You can control the height and width of a textarea field. Instead of pixels, the width is expressed as character width, and height is expressed as the number of lines. Textarea fields are meant to collect long strings of text. When the text exceeds the width of the field, the textarea element wraps the text to the next line.

Text fields

Text fields collect a single line of text. You can control the width of a text field as well as the number of characters that a user can enter. To insert a text field or a textarea field, place the insertion point on the page and click the appropriate button in the Insert bar or drag the appropriate button to the page.

You can convert a text field to a textarea field and vice versa, if you need to make changes as you develop a form. In the Property inspector, click Single line to convert a textarea field to a text field automatically. Click Multi line to convert a text field to a textarea field.

Naming form input fields

Every form input field you create must be given a name so that the information a user enters is submitted to the server as a name/value pair. For example, if you name a text input field `FirstName`, and a user enters the name "Joe" and submits the form, the data `FirstName="Joe"` is submitted for processing. To name a field, select the field and enter a name in the Property inspector.

Do it!

A-2: Inserting text fields into a form

Here's how	Here's why
1 Drag [text field icon] to the cell next to First name, as shown	
	(The Text Field button is in the Forms tab on the Insert bar.) To insert a text field in the form. The Input Tag Accessibility Attributes dialog box appears. Text that you enter in the Label box will appear as a label for the text field on the page. In this case, labels are already on the page. You'll change the preferences so that the dialog box doesn't appear again.

2 Click as shown

> If you don't want to enter this information when
> inserting objects, change the Accessibility preferences.

To open the Preferences dialog box, with the Accessibility category active.

3 Clear **Form objects**

Click **OK**

To close the Preferences dialog box.

Click **OK**

The text field appears next to the First name prompt.

4 Point to the text field and start dragging the text field to the next row, as shown

ame:	
ame:	

(Don't release the mouse button yet.) You'll copy this text field into the other cells, rather than insert each text field with the Text Field button. This is an alternative, not a requirement. Later, you'll give each field a unique name to distinguish among them.

As you drag, press and hold (CTRL)

In the cell below, release the mouse button, then release (CTRL)

To copy the text field into the empty cell.

5 Insert text fields for the remaining prompts, as shown

Personal information

First name:	
Last name:	
Phone:	
Address:	
Address 2:	
City:	
State/Province:	
Zip/Postal Code:	
Country:	
Email:	

Leave the cell next to the Country prompt empty for now.

6 Click the first text field	(In the First name row.) You'll assign each field a unique name. If you don't enter a name, Dreamweaver will generate one automatically.
In the Property inspector, in the TextField box, enter **FirstName**	
	To name the field.
Assign unique and appropriate names to the remaining fields	
7 Click the First name field	You'll change the width of this and other fields.
In the Property inspector, in the Char width box, enter **30**	To increase the width of the text field.
8 Make the Last name, Phone, Address, Address 2, and Email fields the same width	
9 Set the width of the City field to **20**	
10 Set the width of the State/Province and Zip/Postal Code fields to **10**	
11 Drag [icon] to the cell below Comments or questions in the table on the right, as shown	(The Textarea button.) To insert a textarea field.
12 Click the textarea field	To select it.
In the Property inspector, in the TextField box, enter **Comments**	To name the text area. The default size for the textarea field is 45 characters wide by 5 lines tall. You'll make the field smaller.
13 Set the width of the textarea field to **33**	In the Property inspector, in the Char width box, enter 33.
Edit the Num lines field to read **2**	To reduce the height from five lines to two.

14 Observe the table cell

Comments or questions:

The height of the table cell automatically increased when you inserted the large textarea field but didn't reduce when you reduced the height of the textarea field. You'll adjust it to fit.

Click to place the insertion point into the cell to the right of the textarea field, as shown

Comments or questions:

Click anywhere on the page outside the table

Comments or questions:

The cell resizes to fit the new size of its content.

15 Save the page and preview it in Internet Explorer

Close the browser

List boxes and menus

Explanation

List boxes and *menus* allow a user to select one or more items from a list. As shown in Exhibit 3-3, a list box displays a fixed number of rows. If the number of items in the list box is greater than the specified height, a scrollbar appears to allow the user to navigate the entire list.

A menu displays only one item at a time, until a user clicks the menu, which displays the entire menu. This arrangement allows you to preserve space on your page. If you have many items in a list, you probably wouldn't want the entire list to appear by default. In a menu, a scroll bar appears only if the list is so long that it occupies the entire screen. Other terms for a menu or list include *pop-up menu* and *dropdown menu*.

Exhibit 3-3: A list box (left) and a menu (right)

To insert a list box or a menu:

1   Place the insertion point on the page and click the List/Menu icon in the Insert bar, or drag the icon to the position on the page.

2   In the Property inspector, enter a name for the form element.

3   Select Menu or List to define the form element type.

4   If List is selected:

- In the Height box, enter the number of lines to display on the page.

- Next to Selections, click Allow multiple, if you want the user to be able to select more than one item in the list.

5   Click List Values and populate the list. The Item Label appears on the page; the Value is passed to the server. Use the arrow buttons to rearrange the order of items.

6   If there's a default selection for this list (for example, the default value might be Select an item from the list), select it in the Initially selected box.

Do it!

A-3: Adding a list box and a menu

Here's how	Here's why
1 Drag [icon] to the empty row in the second table, as shown	Which publ or Shift clic [dropdown] Would you (The List/Menu button.) To create a list box.
2 Click the list box	To select it and display its options in the Property inspector.
In the List/Menu box, enter **Publications**	▼ Properties List/Menu Publications To name the list box.
Next to Type, select **List**	To make a list rather than a menu. A list displays all of the list items in a box with a scrollbar, depending on the number of items and height of the list box. A menu displays a dropdown list, showing only one selection at a time.
In the Height box, enter **3**	Three options are visible in the box.
Next to Selections, check **Allow multiple**	To allow more than one selection.
3 Click **List Values**	To open the List Values dialog box. By default, the list box contains one item, and it's selected by default.
In the Item Label field, enter **Newsletter**	[+][–] Item Label Value Newsletter This text appears in the list box as the first item.
Press (TAB)	To input a value to associate with this item label.
4 In the Value field, enter **news**	To assign a value to the Newsletter item. This value won't be visible to the user, but it'll be passed to the database if the user selects Newsletter.

5 Press TAB	To enter a new item label.
Enter **Pocket spice guide**	
Press TAB	
Enter **pocketguide**	Values must not contain spaces.
6 Create a third item with the label **Complete spice catalog**	
Set its value to **catalog**	
Click **OK**	To close the List Values dialog box.
7 Observe the list box	The width of the list box expands to accommodate the widest item label.
8 Drag the List/Menu button next to Country, as shown	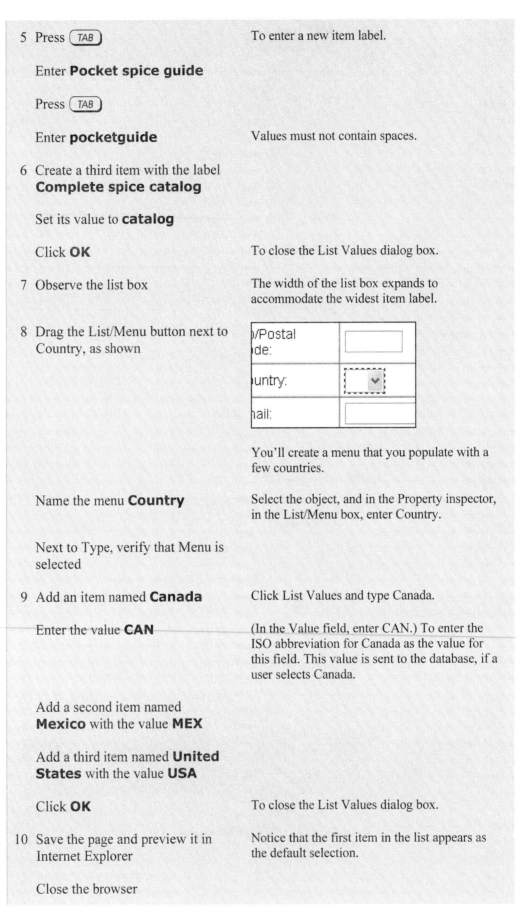
	You'll create a menu that you populate with a few countries.
Name the menu **Country**	Select the object, and in the Property inspector, in the List/Menu box, enter Country.
Next to Type, verify that Menu is selected	
9 Add an item named **Canada**	Click List Values and type Canada.
Enter the value **CAN**	(In the Value field, enter CAN.) To enter the ISO abbreviation for Canada as the value for this field. This value is sent to the database, if a user selects Canada.
Add a second item named **Mexico** with the value **MEX**	
Add a third item named **United States** with the value **USA**	
Click **OK**	To close the List Values dialog box.
10 Save the page and preview it in Internet Explorer	Notice that the first item in the list appears as the default selection.
Close the browser	

11	Expand the Property inspector	(If necessary.) To view the Initially selected option. You'll make United States the default selection.
	In the Initially selected box, select **United States**	Initially selected: Canada / Mexico / United States
12	Save the page and preview it in Internet Explorer	The default selection is now United States.
	Close the browser	

Check boxes and radio buttons

Explanation

Check boxes allow a user to select one or more items. Radio buttons are usually grouped to allow only one selection, so that clicking one radio button clears the others in its group. For example, you'd want to use radio buttons to obtain gender information, because the two options are mutually exclusive.

Creating check boxes

To insert a check box:

1 Place the insertion point on the page and click the Checkbox icon in the Insert bar, or drag the icon to the desired location on the page.
2 In the Property inspector, enter a unique name for the form element.
3 In the Checked value box, enter the value to be passed to the Web server when the box is checked.
4 Select Checked or Unchecked to set the check box's default state.

When entering values for your check box items, think of how the data are to be submitted to the server. In many cases, it makes sense to give check boxes a Yes value. For example, if a series of check boxes is meant to obtain user preferences, you might write options such as "send me coupons" (with a field name of Coupons) and "send me information on future contests and promotions" (with a field name of Promos). By giving both of these check boxes Yes values, the information sent to the server is `coupons="yes"` and/or `promos="yes"`. If they're unchecked, no data are passed, so it isn't necessary to create No values.

Creating radio buttons

To insert a radio button:

1 Place the insertion point on the page and click the Radio Button icon in the Insert bar, or drag the icon to the desired location on the page.
2 In the Property inspector, enter a name for the form element.
3 In the Checked value box, enter the value to be passed to the Web server when the radio button is selected.
4 Select Checked or Unchecked to set the radio button's default state.

All radio buttons that have the same name are members of the same group. That is, when one is checked, it clears all the others, making it impossible to select more than one radio button at a time.

A-4: Adding check boxes and radio buttons

Here's how	Here's why
1 Drag ☑ to the left of Cooking, as shown	
	(The Checkbox button.) To insert a check box.
Name the check box **Cooking**	In the Property inspector, in the Checkbox name box, enter cooking.
2 In the Checked value box, enter **yes**	If a user checks this box, this value will be sent to the database.
3 Insert a check box to the left of the word Baking	From the Insert bar, drag the Checkbox button to the left of the word.
Set its name to **Baking**	
Set its value to **yes**	
4 Drag ⦿ to the left of the words In printed form, as shown	
	(The Radio Button icon.) To insert the first of a pair of mutually exclusive radio buttons.
Name the radio button **InfoFormat**	In the Property inspector, in the Radio Button box, enter InfoFormat.
In the Checked value box, enter **print**	
5 Insert a radio button to the left of the word Delivered	
Name the radio button **InfoFormat**	To give it the same name as the radio button you created previously, making them mutually exclusive.
In the Checked value box, enter **electronic**	
6 Save the page and preview it in Internet Explorer	

7 Check **Cooking**	
Check **Baking**	The check boxes aren't mutually exclusive, so you can select both of them.
8 Click one radio button, and then the other	The radio buttons are mutually exclusive; selecting one radio button clears the other.
9 Type some text in the Comments field	To test the functionality of the textarea field. The text automatically wraps to the next line when it reaches the end.
10 Close the browser	Next, you'll add submit and reset buttons to the form.

Submit and reset buttons

Explanation

Without a submit button, a Web form isn't truly functional. A submit button allows users to submit their information for processing and storage in a database. A reset button allows users to clear all form fields, if they need to start from scratch.

To add a submit or reset button:

1 Place the insertion point on the page and click the Button icon in the Insert bar or drag the icon to the desired location on the page.

2 In the Property inspector, next to Action, select Submit form, Reset form, or None.

3 Enter a unique name for the button.

A-5: Inserting submit and reset buttons

Here's how	Here's why
1 Click to place the insertion point within the cell to the right of the textarea field, as shown	Comments or questions:
Press ⏎ ENTER	To create a space below the field. You'll create a button that submits the form.
2 Drag ⬜ to the area under the field	Submit
	(The Button icon.) To add a Submit button.
In the Property inspector, in the Value box, enter **Send**	The default text label for a button is Submit, but you can change that, as needed.
Verify that Submit form is selected	
3 Drag ⬜ to the right of the Send button	You'll also create a reset button.
In the Button name box, enter **Reset**	
In the Value box, enter **Clear form**	
Next to Action, select **Reset form**	Action ○ Submit form ◉ Reset form
4 Save the page and preview it in Internet Explorer	
Fill out some of the form fields	
Click **Clear form**	All the form entries are cleared.
5 Close the browser	To return to Dreamweaver.
6 Close the document	

Topic B: Form accessibility

This topic covers the following Adobe ACE exam objective for Dreamweaver CS3.

#	Objective
2.7	List and describe the features Dreamweaver provides for Accessibility Standards/Section 508 compliance.

Explanation

Users can navigate through form fields by pressing Tab. Sometimes the default tab order of a form, particularly if the form is set in a table, isn't the best or intended sequence. You can customize the tab order to enhance usability and accessibility.

Tab order

The tab order is the order in which the insertion point jumps from input field to input field as the user presses Tab. Sometimes, the forms you create might already have a logical tab order without having to specify one manually. It's often a good idea to specify a logical order anyway, to ensure that users with screen readers and other assistive devices are able to interact with the form optimally.

Do it!

B-1: Observing the default tab order

Here's how	Here's why
1 Open orderonline.html	The document shows a simple form for ordering products online.
2 Preview the page in Internet Explorer	
3 In the Billing section, select a card type from the Card Type list	You'll test the default tab order in this section of the form.
Press (TAB)	The insertion point moves to the Full Name field.
Press (TAB)	The insertion point moves to the Card No field.
4 In this particular form, is the default tab order logical?	
5 Close the browser	

Setting the tab order of input fields

Explanation

The default tab order is set according to the order in which the fields occur in the code. This might not result in a logical flow from one input field to the next. You should specify your intended tab order to enhance the usability and accessibility of your forms.

To define the tab order of a form input field:

1   Right-click the field and select Edit Tag. The Tag Editor dialog box appears.

2   Select Style Sheet/Accessibility to view the options in that category.

3   In the Tab Index box, enter the number that represents the field's position in the sequence.

4   Click OK to close the dialog box.

To make an input field the first field in a tabbing sequence, enter the number 1 in the Tab Index box. Proceed through 2, 3, and so on for each field, as needed. If you set a tab order, be sure to set Tab Index values for *all* form fields. Otherwise, the tab order might not follow a logical sequence.

Do it!

B-2: Setting the tab order

Here's how	Here's why
1 Right-click the Card Type field	You'll change the tab order, so that all the fields in the Billing section are selected before the fields in the Shipping section.
Choose **Edit Tag <select>...**	To open the Tag Editor dialog box.
2 Select **Style Sheet/Accessibility**	
In the Tab index box, enter **1** and click **OK**	You'll assign tab numbers for the rest of the form fields.
3 Set the Tab index for the Card No field to **2**	Right-click the field, choose Edit Tag <input>, select Style Sheet/Accessibility, enter 2 in the Tab index box, and click OK.
4 Set the Tab index fields for the Exp Date and Security Code fields	Set them to 3 and 4, respectively.
5 Set the tab order for the Shipping section	Begin by setting the Full Name field tab index to 5, and then number the remaining fields sequentially.
6 Set the tab order for the Product section	Begin by setting the first QTY field tab index to 10, then number the fields left to right sequentially.
7 Save the page and preview it in Internet Explorer	
8 In the Billing section, select a card type from the Card Type list	
9 Press (TAB)	The insertion point moves to the Card No field.
Press (TAB)	The insertion point moves to the Exp Date field.
10 Close the browser	
11 Close all open files	

Unit summary: Forms

Topic A   In this topic, you learned how to create an **interactive form**. You learned how to add **text fields**, **textarea** fields, **lists**, **menus**, **check boxes**, and **radio buttons**. You also learned how to set **input field properties**, such as height and width, by using the Property inspector. Finally, you learned how to create **submit** and **reset buttons**.

Topic B   In this topic, you learned how to improve the accessibility of your forms by defining a **tab order**. You learned that, by default, the tab order is set according to the order in which input fields appear in the code.

Independent practice activity

In this activity, you'll create a form by placing existing content within form tags. Then you'll add form elements and set values for them. Finally, you'll define a tab order and test the form in a browser.

1 Create a new site named **Forms practice** by using the Outlander folder inside the Practice folder as the local root folder. (The Practice folder is located in the current unit folder.)

2 Open create_login.html.

3 In the rowTop div, click the `<h1>` tag in the tag selector at the bottom of the document window. (*Hint*: Place the insertion point in the heading, "Request for information," then click the `<h1>` tag.)

4 Choose **Edit**, **Cut** (or press Ctrl+X).

5 Insert a new form in the rowTop DIV. (*Hint*: In the Insert bar, click the Form icon.)

6 Paste the headline in the form, and press Enter.

7 Cut and paste the two tables into the form. (*Hint*: The tables are contained in the formLeft and formRight DIVs. Select each DIV, cut it, and paste it into the form.)

8 Add text fields for the First name, Last name, Email, Login name, and Password rows. Give each field a unique name.

9 Add radio buttons to the left of the Male and Female options. Give the radio buttons the same name, so that selecting one clears the other. In the Property inspector, enter appropriate text in the Checked value box.

10 Insert a menu in the cell below the question "Where did you first hear of Outlander Spices?" To do so, drag the List/Menu button from the Insert bar. Select the menu. In the Property inspector, next to Type, select **Menu**.

11 Add the following items to the menu: **Select one**, **Grocery store**, **Gourmet shop**, **The Web**, **A friend**. Assign a unique value to each selection. (*Hint*: In the Property inspector, click **List Values**.)

12 In the Property inspector, in the Initially selected box, select **Select one** to make it the default selection.

13 Insert check boxes before the choices, **Online** and **In grocery stores**, and give each a unique name and checked value.

14 Insert a textarea field in the row below **Comments or questions**. Set its width to 35 or less.

15 At the bottom of the right table, insert two buttons. Name one **Reset** and the other **Send**.

16 Make the Reset button to reset the form fields. To do so, select the Reset button. In the Property inspector, next to Action, select **Reset form**.

17 Define a logical tab order to every form field and the Reset and Send buttons. As you click each form element, verify that it has a unique name and value.

18 Preview the page in Internet Explorer and test the tab order.

19 Save and close the page.

Review questions

1 True or False? If you define the tab order for one or more input fields, you should define the tab order for *all* input fields.

2 The default tab order of a set of form input fields is determined by:

A The default Tab Index values that Dreamweaver automatically applies to each input field.

B The order in which the input fields appear in a browser.

C The order in which the input fields appear in the code.

D Alphabetical order.

3 To start a form, you need to:

A Add input fields.

B Insert a form container by dragging the Form icon to the page or by clicking the Form icon while the insertion point is positioned on the page.

C Clear all other HTML first.

D Switch to Code or Split view.

4 Every form input field you create must be given a name, so that:

A You can keep track of each form field.

B Users can more easily navigate the form.

C The tab order follows a logical sequence.

D The information a user enters is submitted to the server as a name/value pair.

5 True or False? All form input fields must be placed inside the <form> container.

6 The main difference between check boxes and radio buttons is:

   A Check boxes are square and radio buttons are round.

   B Radio buttons are meant to offer mutually exclusive options, and check boxes aren't.

   C Check boxes aren't usually checked by default.

   D Radio buttons aren't usually selected by default.

7 True or False? Without a submit button, a Web form isn't truly functional.

Unit 4

Rollovers and behaviors

Unit time: 30 minutes

Complete this unit, and you'll know how to:

A Create a navigation bar using rollover images.

B Add the Swap Image behavior to control other images on the page, and open a new browser window.

Topic A: Rollovers

This topic covers the following Adobe ACE exam objectives for Dreamweaver CS3.

#	Objective
1.3	Explain how JavaScript is used on the client in Web pages.
3.17	Given a coding tool or features, describe the purpose of or how to use that tool or feature.

JavaScript

JavaScript is a scripting language that you can use to add interactivity and functionality to your Web pages. For example, the rollovers and behaviors that you create in Dreamweaver are made with JavaScript code, as shown in Exhibit 4-1.

```
      <td><a href="javascript:;" target="_top" onclick=
"MM_nbGroup('down','group1','bayleaf','',1)" onmouseover=
"MM_nbGroup('over','bayleaf','images/bayleaftextglow.gif','',1)" onmouseout="MM_nbGroup('out')">
<img src="images/bayleaftext.gif" alt="" name="bayleaf" width="115" height="30" border="0" id=
"bayleaf" onload="" /></a></td>
```

Exhibit 4-1: Javascript code that creates a rollover

If you want a script to apply to multiple pages, you can create an external JavaScript file and link the pages to it, similar to the way pages are linked to an external style sheet.

If you want to write your own JavaScripts, you'll find many Web sites on the Internet that offer basic JavaScript tutorials. Many of these sites include a variety of free sample scripts that you can use in your Web site.

You can use *Code Navigation* to locate JavaScript or Vbscript functions quickly and easily within your code while working in Code view or the Code Inspector. To navigate to a function in Code View:

1   Switch to Code view.
2   Right-click within the code and choose Functions, as shown in Exhibit 4-2. A submenu appears.
3   Select the desired function from the list.
4   Code view navigates to the start of that function and highlights its name.

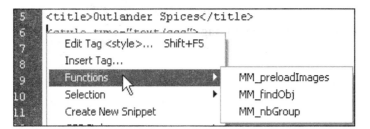

Exhibit 4-2: Code Navigation within Code view.

To navigate to a function while working in the Code Inspector, click the Code Navigation button, and then choose a function.

Rollover images

A *rollover* swaps a *primary image*, the original image on the page, with a *secondary image*. A rollover can be triggered by many user actions, called *events*. This type of interactivity is popular, because it provides visual feedback for a user's actions.

The rollover function is achieved using JavaScript. Dreamweaver writes the required JavaScript code automatically, so you don't have to learn the programming part of it. Pointing to the primary image is the most common user event, and Dreamweaver uses this as the default event for rollovers.

The primary and secondary images should be the same size, in terms of height and width. File sizes can be different, but the dimensions of the two images should be identical to prevent distortion and to create a smooth transition between the primary and secondary images.

To create a rollover:

1　Place the insertion point on the page.

2　On the Insert bar, select the Common category.

3　Click the black triangle next to the Images button and select Rollover Image. The Insert Rollover Image dialog box opens.

4　In the Image name box, enter a name for the rollover.

5　Next to the Original image box, click Browse and select the primary image.

6　Next to the Rollover image box, click Browse and select the secondary image.

7　Verify that Preload rollover image is checked.

8　Enter alternate text, which appears if the browser can't display the image(s). Alternate text can also be read by screen readers and other assistive devices.

9　Click OK.

10　(Optional) In the Behaviors panel, click onMouseOver and select a different triggering event from the list to replace the default.

Navigation bars

Rollovers are most commonly used to create link buttons in navigation bars. Dreamweaver makes it quick and easy to create rollover navigation bars. Rollovers consist of the following images:

- **Up image:** The image that appears when the rollover is in its default state, and no event has been triggered.

- **Over image:** The image that appears when the user points to the Up image. When this event is triggered, the Over image replaces the Up image.

- **Down image:** The image that appears when the user clicks the Over image.

- **Over while down image:** The image that appears when the user points to the rollover after it has been clicked.

To create a navigation bar:

1   Place the insertion point on the page.

2   In the Insert bar, select the Common category.

3   Click the black triangle next to the Images button and select Navigation Bar. The Insert Navigation Bar dialog box opens.

4   In the Element name box, enter a name for the first item in the navigation bar.

5   Next to the Up image box, click Browse and select the primary image.

6   Next to the Over image box, click Browse and select the secondary image.

7   (Optional) Next to the Down image box, click Browse and select an image to display when the user clicks the secondary image.

8   (Optional) Next to the Over while down image box, click Browse and select an image to display when the user points to an item that has been clicked.

9   Enter alternate text for text-only browsers, screen readers, and other assistive devices.

10   In the When clicked, Go to URL box, enter the URL or path of the destination page or resource.

11   Verify that Preload images is checked.

12   From the Insert list, select the direction (Vertically or Horizontally) that you want the navigation bar to extend.

13   Click the Add item button, and repeat these steps for the remaining buttons in the navigation bar.

14   Use the Move item in list buttons to arrange the order of the navigation items, if necessary.

15   Click OK.

Do it!

A-1: Creating a navigation bar with rollover images

Here's how	Here's why
1 Choose **Site, New Site...**	
2 Edit the Site name box to read **Outlander rollovers**	In the Advanced tab.
In the Local root folder box, navigate to the Outlander folder	In the current unit folder.
Click **Select**	
Click **OK**	To define the site.
3 Open gallery.html	You'll create a navigation bar with rollover images.
4 Triple-click the text shown	
	To select it.
Press (DELETE)	
5 Activate the Common tab on the Insert bar	
6 Click as shown	
	To display the image options.
Choose **Navigation Bar**	To open the Insert Navigation Bar dialog box. You'll create several rollover images, which Dreamweaver will arrange in a navigation bar.
Edit the Element name box to read **bayleaf**	

7	Next to the Up image box, click **Browse**	To open the Select image source dialog box.
	Select **bayleaftext.gif**	In the images folder, in the Outlander folder.
	Click **OK**	
8	Next to the Over image box, click **Browse**	
	Select **bayleaftextglow.gif**	
	Click **OK**	
9	Click [+]	(The Add item button.) An item named unnamed1 appears in the Nav bar elements list under bayleaf.
	Type **cloves**	To rename the new item.
	For the Up image, select **clovestext.gif**	In the images folder, in the Outlander folder.
	For the Over image, select **clovestextglow.gif**	
10	Add the Nav bar element **cinnamon**	Click the Add item button, and type cinnamon. Add the cinnamontext.gif and cinnamontextglow.gif images, respectively, to the Up image and Over image boxes.
	Click [▲]	(The Move item up in list button.) Cinnamon should come before cloves, to arrange the list alphabetically.
11	Verify that Preload images is checked	So that the images loads when the page opens, rather than when the mouse pointer moves over the rollover image. If this isn't checked, the user might see a delay while the image loads.
12	From the Insert list, select **Vertically**	
	Click **OK**	To add the navigation bar to the page.
13	Save the page and preview it in Internet Explorer	
14	Point to the spice names	When the pointer moves over an image, the image changes to the Over image, creating the illusion that the text itself is changing. When the pointer moves off the spice name, the image reverts to the original.
	Close the browser	

15	Switch to Code view	You'll observe the JavaScript that performs the rollovers.
16	Right-click within the code and choose **Functions**, **MM_nbGroup**	To navigate to that JavaScript function.
	Observe the JavaScript code	
	Switch to Design view	

Topic B: Behaviors

This topic covers the following Adobe ACE exam objective for Dreamweaver CS3.

#	Objective
2.10	Explain how to extend Dreamweaver by using Extensions.

Using behaviors

Explanation

Behaviors allow a user to interact with your Web page in a variety of ways. Behaviors are a combination of an *event*, which is typically triggered by the user, and an *action*, which occurs in response to the event. Behaviors are embedded in your Web page as blocks of JavaScript code.

To attach a behavior to an object:

1 Select an object serve as the event trigger on the page.
2 In the Behaviors panel, click the Add behavior button and select a behavior from the menu. A dialog box specific to that behavior opens.
3 Use the fields and controls in the dialog box to define the behavior.
4 Click OK.

The Swap Image behavior

The *Swap Image* behavior uses a trigger event to cause changes to one or more other images on the page. The trigger object itself doesn't change, unless the trigger object has been assigned its own rollover event.

To apply a Swap Image behavior:

1 Select the image on the page to serve as the trigger object.
2 In the Behaviors panel, click the Add behavior button and choose Swap Image. The Swap Image dialog box opens, as shown in Exhibit 4-3.
3 From the Images list, select the image on the page to be replaced.
4 Next to the Set source to box, click Browse and select a secondary image.
5 Verify that Preload images is checked.
6 Verify that Restore images onMouseOut is checked.
7 Click OK.

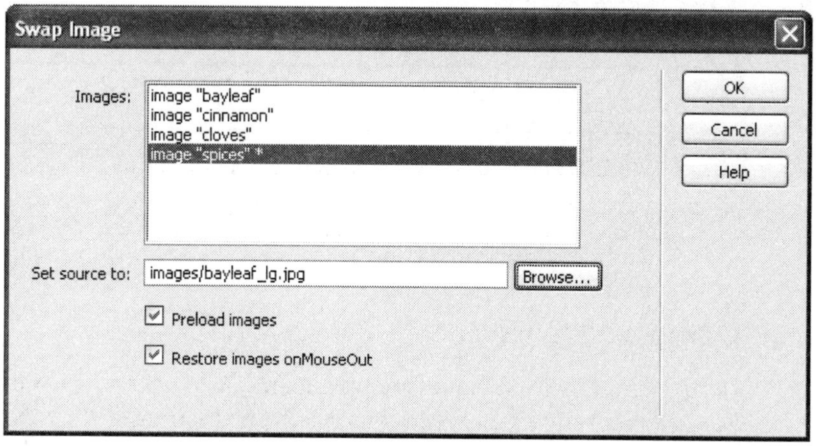

Exhibit 4-3: The Swap Image dialog box

B-1: Applying the Swap Image behavior

Here's how	Here's why
1 In the gallery page, click the Bayleaf text image	To select it. You'll add a swap image action to the spice names, so that their corresponding images appear in place of the current spice image on the page.
2 Activate the Behaviors panel	(Choose Window, Behaviors.) Three actions are already associated with the image. Dreamweaver added these when you created the rollover images.
Click [+,]	The Add behavior button.
Choose **Swap Image**	To open the Swap Image dialog box.
3 From the Images list, select **image "spices"**	To select the image of the spices currently on the page.
Next to the Set source to box, click **Browse**	To open the Select Image Source dialog box.
Select **bayleaf_lg.jpg**	(In the images folder, in the Outlander folder.) To replace the spices image with a large image of bay leaves.
Click **OK**	An asterisk appears next to image "spices" in the Images list, indicating that an action has been applied.
4 Verify that Preload images is checked	
Verify that Restore images onMouseOut is checked	
Click **OK**	To close the dialog box and add the action. In the Behaviors panel, Dreamweaver has added the Swap Image and the Swap Image Restore actions.
5 Click the Cinnamon text image	To select it.
6 Add the Swap Image behavior to the image	In the Behaviors panel, click the Add behavior button, and choose Swap Image.
Swap the spices image with cinnamon_lg.jpg	In the Images list, select image "spices." Click Browse, and select cinnamon_lg.jpg.
Click **OK**	
Click **OK**	

7 Add a swap image action to the Cloves text image

Swap the spice image with the cloves_lg.jpg image

8 Save the page and preview it in Internet Explorer

Point to the spice names

The corresponding images appear when the mouse moves over each spice name. The default image is displayed when the pointer isn't over one of the images.

Close the browser

9 Close gallery.html

Opening a link in a new browser window

Explanation

The Open Browser Window behavior lets you open any URL in a new browser window. You can also set attributes for the new browser window, such as its size and the type of navigation controls it includes. You can use the behavior to show an enlarged image of a product or to open multimedia, such as video clips or animations.

To add the Open Browser Window behavior:

1 Select the object you want to use for the trigger.

2 In the Behaviors panel, click the Add behavior button and choose Open Browser Window. The Open Browser Window dialog box opens, as shown Exhibit 4-4.

3 In the URL to display box, enter the path and filename for the page to be opened.

4 In the Window width and Window height boxes, enter values to determine the size of the new window.

5 Next to Attributes, select the window attributes you want to include, such as the navigation toolbar, status bar, or scrollbars. By default, all options are deselected.

6 In the Window name box, enter a unique name or ID for the window. (You can use the window name to apply CSS styles or target the window with links).

7 Click OK.

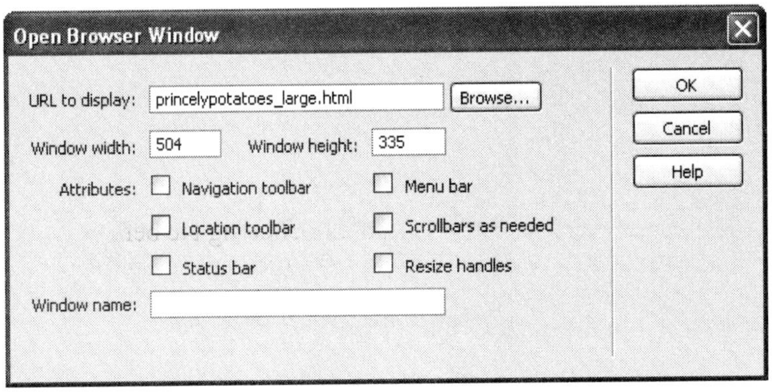

Exhibit 4-4: The Open Browser Window dialog box

Editing behaviors

By default, most behaviors use the onClick event to trigger the behavior action. This means that the behavior action doesn't occur until a user clicks the object to which the behavior is applied. Often though, you'll want to change the behavior event to something else, such as onMouseOver or onMouseOut.

To change behavior events:

1   In the Behaviors panel, select the behavior for which you want to change the trigger event.

2   To the right of the event, click the down arrow to expand the Event list.

3   Select a new trigger event from the list, as shown in Exhibit 4-5.

Exhibit 4-5: Adjusting a trigger event in the Behaviors panel

You can also edit behaviors by double-clicking the behavior in the Action column. Double-clicking the behavior opens the corresponding dialog box.

B-2: Applying the Open Browser Window behavior

Here's how	Here's why
1 Open princelypotatoes.html	You want users to be able to see a larger view of the princely potatoes image when they click it. You'll add a behavior that opens the larger image in a new browser window.
2 Click the potatoes image	To select it. Before you apply the behavior, you should create a blank link for the image.
3 In the Property inspector, in the Link box, enter **#**	To create a blank link.
4 In the Behaviors panel, click ➕▾	The Add behavior button.
Choose **Open Browser Window**	To open the Open Browser Window dialog box.
5 Click **Browse**	The Select File dialog box appears.
Select **princelypototoes_large.html**	
Click **OK**	To close the Select File dialog box.
6 In the Window width box, enter **504**	
In the Window height box, enter **335**	URL to display: princelypotatoes_large.html Window width: 504 Window height: 335
7 Observe the checkboxes	By default, all the checkboxes are cleared. Because you don't want any navigational elements in the new window, you'll leave them as they are.
8 Click **OK**	To close the dialog box.
9 Save the page and preview it in Internet Explorer	
Point to the potatoes image	When you point to it, the pointer changes to a pointing finger, indicating that the image is a link.
Click the image	A new smaller browser window opens, showing the larger potatoes image. The window doesn't have any navigational elements, so the only thing viewers can do after they view the image is close the window.

10 Close the new browser

   Close the browser

11 Close princelypotatoes.html

Dreamweaver extensions

Some page elements, such as flyout or pop-up menus, require advanced JavaScript knowledge to code properly. Instead of coding by hand, you can download third-party plug-in extensions from the online Exchange site. (To download from the Exchange site, you must register as an Adobe user and create a username and password for the site.) The plug-ins enhance Dreamweaver's functionality by adding new commands and wizards to the interface. Often, they allow you to perform complex tasks without needing to work directly within the code.

To download a plug-in extension:

1   Choose Commands, Manage Extensions to open the Adobe Extension Manager.

2   Choose File, Go To Adobe Exchange. The Adobe Exchange site opens in a browser. The site shows a list of available extensions divided into categories. Some are free, and others are offered for sale. Any extensions you download are automatically installed and become visible in the Extension Manager, as shown in Exhibit 4-6.

3   Click the Download button beside an extension. The Adobe site prompts you to sign in.

4   If you're a returning Adobe customer, enter your e-mail address and password. If not, follow the instructions to create one now.

5   After you sign in, the Dreamweaver Exchange page appears again. An Extension Download License window appears.

6   Click Accept.

7   Click the Download button beside an extension to download it. The File Download dialog box appears.

8   Click Save. The Save As dialog box appears.

9   Navigate to the desired folder and click Save. The Download dialog box indicates that the Download is complete.

10 Click Close to close the dialog box.

11 Close the browser.

12 In the Adobe Extension dialog box, choose File, Install Extension.

13 Navigate to the folder where you downloaded the extension.

14 Select the extension and click Install. The Adobe Extension Manager dialog box appears.

15 Click Accept. The extension installs. The Adobe Extension Manager dialog box prompts you to restart Dreamweaver.

16 Click OK to close the dialog box.

17 Click Accept. The extension installs. The Adobe Extension Manager dialog box prompts you to restart Dreamweaver.

To deactivate an extension, clear the checkbox to the left of the extension in the On/Off column. Each time you install or deactivate an extension, you must close and restart Dreamweaver for the action to take effect.

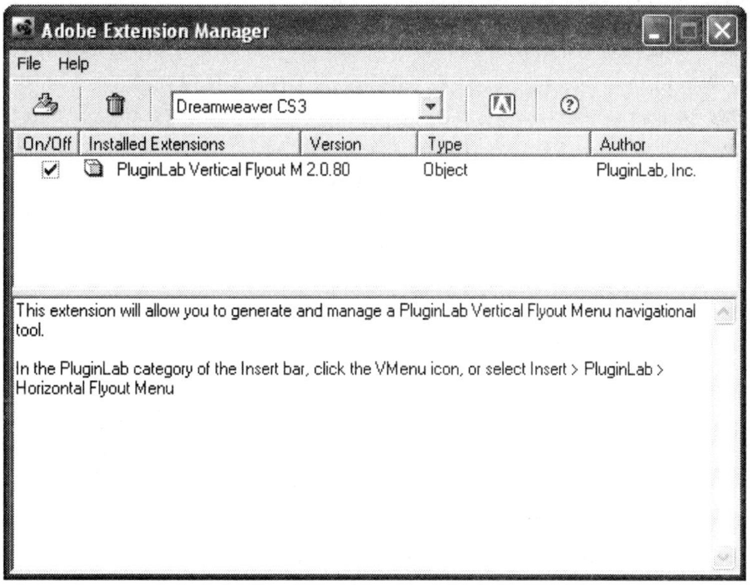

Exhibit 4-6: The Adobe Extension Manager

Do it!

B-3:   Exploring Dreamweaver extensions

Here's how	Here's why
1 Choose **Commands**, **Manage Extensions...**	To open the Adobe Extension Manager. You'll observe some of the extensions that are available for download.
2 In the Adobe Extension Manager, choose **File**, **Go To Adobe Exchange**	To open the Adobe Exchange page in a browser.
3 Under Exchanges by product, click **Dreamweaver**	To view the Dreamweaver Exchange page.
4 Scroll through the list of available extensions and read some of the descriptions	
5 Close the browser Close the Adobe Extension Manager	

Unit summary: Rollovers and behaviors

Topic A

In this topic, you learned about **rollover images**. You learned that rollovers are a popular design technique, because they provide visual feedback for a user's actions. You also learned how to create a **navigation bar** with rollovers.

Topic B

In this topic, you learned how to use the **swap image** behavior to control other images on the page, and you learned how to use the **Open Browser Window behavior** to open a new browser window when users click a link. Finally, you learned how to access third-party plug-in **extensions** to enhance Dreamweaver's functionality.

Independent practice activity

In this activity, you'll edit an existing navigation bar by adding some new elements to it. Then you'll apply the Swap Image behavior to the new navigation bar elements.

1 Create a new site named **Rollovers practice**, using the Outlander folder inside the Practice folder as the local root folder.

2 Open gallery.html.

3 In the Insert bar, click the Images : Navigation Bar button. An alert dialog box appears. Click **OK** to edit the navigation bar. (If the Navigation option of the Images button isn't active, click the Images button to display the list of options and select Navigation Bar.)

4 Add the element, coriander, to the end of the list. To do so, in the Nav bar elements list, select **cloves**. Then click the plus-sign icon to add a new element to the end of the list.

5 For the coriander element, select **coriandertext.gif** as the Up image and **coriandertextglow.gif** as the Over image.

6 Add the elements, cumin and pepper, to the end of the list, and select the appropriate Up image and Over image for each.

7 Click **OK** to add the elements to the navigation bar.

8 For each new element, add a Swap Image action that replaces the placeholder image with images of the appropriate spice when the mouse rolls over the spice's name. To do so, click a spice name image to select it. In the Behaviors panel, add a swap image action. In the Swap Image dialog box, in the Images list, select **image "spices"** and browse to the appropriate spice image. For Coriander, Cumin, and Pepper, use the coriander_lg.jpg, cumin_lg.jpg, and pepper.jpg images.

9 Preview the page in Internet Explorer to verify that the rollovers work as expected.

10 Close the browser.

11 Close gallery.html.

Review questions

1 A rollover is triggered by a(n):

 A Behavior

 B Up image

 C Over image

 D Event

2 True or false? The primary and secondary images of a rollover should have the same height and width.

3 What's the difference between a rollover image and a swap image behavior?

4 Behaviors are a combination of:

 A An event and a user-triggered event.

 B An event and an action.

 C An event and a rollover.

 D A rollover and a swap image.

5 How can you attach a behavior to an object?

 A Double-click an object on the page, then select a behavior, and click OK.

 B Select an object on the page, then choose Modify, Image Properties. Select a behavior, and click OK.

 C Select an object on the page. In the Property inspector, click Behaviors. Select a behavior, and click OK.

 D Select an object on the page. In the Behaviors panel, click the Add behavior button and select a behavior from the menu.

6 Which behavior uses a trigger event to cause changes to one or more other images on the page.

 A Go To URL

 B Swap Image

 C Change Property

 D Pop-Up Menus

7   When using the Open Browser Window behavior, which attributes for window can you control within the Open Browser Window dialog box? (Choose all that apply.)

A   Where the window opens on the screen.

B   The width and height of the window.

C   Whether toolbars, resize handles, or scroll bars are visible.

D   The color of the window.

8   How can you open the Adobe Extension Manager?

A   Choose Commands, Manage Extensions.

B   In the Behaviors panel, click the Extension Manager button.

C   Choose Window, Components.

D   Choose View, Plug-Ins.

Unit 5

AP elements

Unit time: 40 minutes

Complete this unit, and you'll know how to:

A Insert AP elements.

B Adjust the size, position, and visibility of an AP Div and control visibility dynamically.

Topic A: AP Divs

This topic covers the following Adobe ACE exam objectives for Dreamweaver CS3.

#	Objective
2.12	Given a scenario, choose the proper method to lay out a page.
3.8	Given a method, lay out a page.
3.11	Lay out a page by using guides.

AP elements

In Dreamweaver CS3, elements that are absolutely positioned with CSS are called *AP elements.* You can place text, images, or any other content, in an AP element. Each AP element has a *z-index* property, which defines its depth relative to other AP elements on the page. (Z-index depth is also called the stacking order. Because AP elements may overlap, the z-index property determines which elements appear on top of others.) The higher the integer value, the higher that AP element appears in the stacking order. You can stack AP elements in layers on your page, with content in one AP element overlapping another, as shown in Exhibit 5-1.

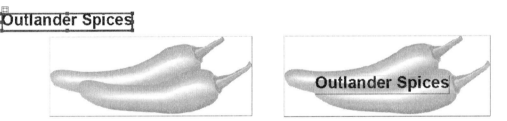

Exhibit 5-1: An AP element overlapping an image (right)

The AP Elements panel

AP elements are usually <div> tags ("AP Divs"), but any element that's absolutely positioned is considered an AP element and will appear in the AP Elements panel. With the AP Elements panel, you can select AP elements, control their stacking order, and set visibility properties. To open the AP elements panel, choose Window, AP Elements. In Design view, you can draw AP Divs directly on a page, then reposition and resize them as needed.

CSS positioning

CSS positioning is a layout method that provides precise control over the arrangement of elements in a layout. There are four types of positioning, as described in the following table.

Option	Description
Absolute	This type positions an element at exact pixel coordinates based on the top, left corner of the browser window. Absolutely positioned elements always remain in their set position within a document, which doesn't change as new content is added or arranged. All absolutely positioned elements appear in the AP Elements panel.
Fixed	Fixed positioning is a subcategory of absolute positioning. The only difference is that a fixed positioned element doesn't scroll with the document—the positioning coordinates are fixed to the browser window.
Relative	This type positions an element relative to its normal location in the document flow. In other words, a relatively positioned element is positioned relative to the location it would normally occupy if it weren't positioned. Relatively positioned elements don't appear in the AP Elements panel.
Static	This is the default positioning option when no positioning is applied. Static positioning displays an element at its normal default location in the document. This is the same as not specifying any positioning value, so it's use is limited to dynamic scripting, where you might need to turn off an element's positioning if certain conditions are met.

Inserting AP Divs

Explanation

AP Divs serve as containers for page content that you can position with pixel-level precision. AP Divs are also called *layers*, because you can stack them on top of each other. This stacking and overlapping ability provides flexibility with your design and content arrangements.

To insert an AP Div, click to place the insertion point where you want it on the page, and then choose Insert, Layout Objects, AP Div. You can also use the Draw AP Div tool. In the Layout tab of the Insert bar, click the Draw AP Div button, and then drag on the page to draw the AP Div. You can also press and hold the Control key to draw multiple AP Divs. Another method you can use is to drag the Draw AP Div button itself onto the page. An AP Div container appears wherever you release the mouse button.

After you've created an AP Div, you can click inside it to place the insertion point, and then add whatever content you need.

When you create an AP Div, Dreamweaver creates a `<div>` tag in the HTML code and assigns a default ID to it. Dreamweaver also writes internal CSS rules, which control the position and dimensions of the AP Div, into the head section of the page. Exhibit 5-2 shows an example of the HTML code that Dreamweaver writes when you create an AP Div, and Exhibit 5-3 shows an example of the corresponding CSS code that controls its size and position.

```
<div id="apDiv1">
Content of apDiv 1...
</div>

<div id="apDiv2">
Content of apDiv 2...
</div>
```

Exhibit 5-2: An example of the HTML code for two AP Divs

```
#apDiv1 {
    position:absolute;
    left:129px;
    top:292px;
    width:226px;
    height:109px;
    z-index:2;
}
#apDiv2 {
    position:absolute;
    width:105px;
    height:64px;
    z-index:3;
    left: 404px;
    top: 485px;
}
```

Exhibit 5-3: An example of absolute positioning rules controlling AP Divs

Guides

Guides are green horizontal and vertical lines you can add to a page to assist with the precise placement of objects. To create guides, drag from either the horizontal or vertical rulers, and position the guide where you want it on the page. Guides don't display in a browser; they appear only in Design view to help you arrange content.

Do it!   **A-1: Inserting AP Divs**

Here's how	**Here's why**
1 Choose **Site**, **New Site...**	
2 On the Advanced tab, name the site **AP elements**	In the Site name box.
In the Local root folder box, open and select the Outlander folder	(In the current unit folder.) To select the Outlander folder as the root folder of the site.
Click **OK**	To create the site. Dreamweaver displays the site in the Files panel.
3 Open heatquiz.html	(From the Files panel.) You'll use AP Divs to create a pop-up heat quiz on this page. You'll begin by adding a large heat graph background image.
Verify that Design view is selected	
4 Point to the horizontal ruler, as shown	
	You'll create a horizontal guide to line up the top of the heat graph image with the pop-up navigation links on the left side of the page.
Drag from the ruler to the top of the navigation links box, as shown	
	To create a horizontal guide.

5   On the Insert bar, activate the
Layout tab

In the Insert bar, click [icon]   The Draw AP Div button.

Drag to create a rectangular
container, as shown

order, from least hot to hottest. Have fun!
Cayenne
Habanero
Chipotle
Pepperonicini
Jalapeno

To create an AP Div.

6   In the Files panel, expand the
images folder

Expand the heatgraph_images
folder

7   Drag heatgraph.jpg into the AP
Div, as shown

order, from least hot to hottest. Have fun!
Cayenne
Habanero
Chipotle
Pepperonicini
Jalapeno

When you release the mouse button, the Image
Tag Accessibility Attributes dialog box appears.

In the Alternate text box, enter
Heat graph

Click **OK**   When you insert an image that's larger than the
                                               AP Div, the container resizes automatically.
                                               Therefore, the size of the container isn't
                                               important when you draw it. You can also resize
                                               it manually, as necessary.

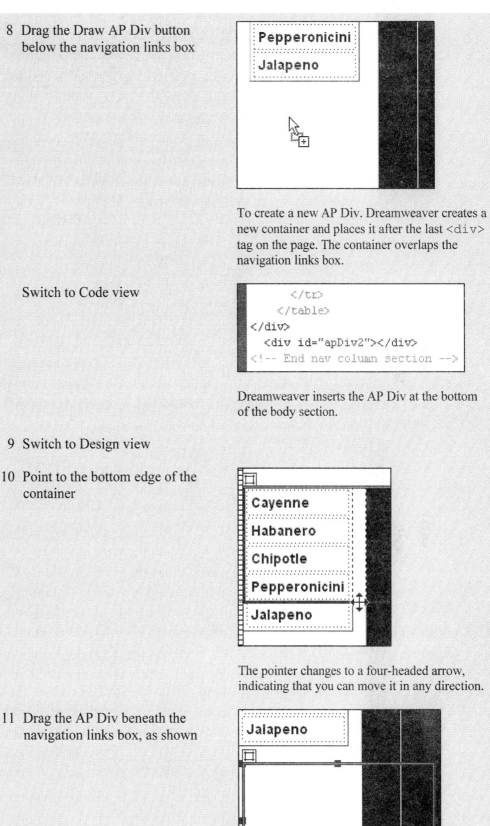

8 Drag the Draw AP Div button below the navigation links box

To create a new AP Div. Dreamweaver creates a new container and places it after the last `<div>` tag on the page. The container overlaps the navigation links box.

Switch to Code view

```
          </tr>
       </table>
</div>
   <div id="apDiv2"></div>
<!-- End nav column section -->
```

Dreamweaver inserts the AP Div at the bottom of the body section.

9 Switch to Design view

10 Point to the bottom edge of the container

The pointer changes to a four-headed arrow, indicating that you can move it in any direction.

11 Drag the AP Div beneath the navigation links box, as shown

12	Drag cayenne.gif into the AP Div	(From the heatgraph_images folder.) The Image Tag Accessibility Attributes dialog box appears.
	In the Alternate text box, type **Cayenne**	
	Click **OK**	
13	Save the document	Next, you'll add more AP Divs, arrange them on the page, and modify their settings.

Topic B: Working with AP Divs

This topic covers the following Adobe ACE exam objective for Dreamweaver CS3.

#	Objective
3.8	Given a method, lay out a page.

Selecting AP Divs

Explanation

After you create an AP Div, you can resize it, move it anywhere on a page, rename it, and apply other properties. You can select one or more AP Divs to change their properties. When an AP Div is selected, you can point to the interior of the container to view its properties. You can also point to its border to view its margin, border, and padding values, and you can also use the Property inspector to view its properties.

To modify an AP Div, you must first select it. You can select an AP Div several ways:

- Click the selection handle of the AP Div.
- Click the border of the AP Div.
- Press Ctrl+Shift and click inside the AP Div.
- Click inside the AP Div and press Ctrl+A.
- Click inside the AP Div and then click its tag in the tag selector.
- In the AP Elements panel, click the AP Div's name.

To select multiple AP Divs, do one of the following:

- Shift-click inside or on the border of two or more AP Divs.
- In the AP Elements panel, Shift-click two or more AP Div names.

Moving an AP Div

To move an AP Div, select it and do one of the following:

- Drag the selection handle.
- Press an arrow key to move the AP Div one pixel at a time.
- Hold down Shift and press an arrow key to move the AP Div one grid increment at a time.

Resizing an AP Div

To resize an AP Div, select it and do one of the following:

- Drag any of the AP Div's resize handles.
- Hold down Ctrl, and press the arrow keys to resize one pixel at a time by moving the right and bottom borders of the AP Div.
- Hold down Shift+Ctrl, and press the arrow keys to resize the grid one increment at a time by moving the right and bottom borders of the AP Div.
- In the Property inspector, enter values in the W and H boxes.

Naming an AP Div

To name an AP Div, do one of the following:

- Select an AP Div, and in the Property inspector in the CSS-P Element box, enter a name.
- In the AP Elements panel, double-click an AP Div name and edit the existing name.

Do it!

B-1: Manipulating AP Divs

Here's how	Here's why
1 Select the heat graph AP Div	
	(Click an edge of the AP Div to select it.) The AP Div is highlighted, and the selection handle appears in the top-left corner. You'll name the new AP Divs, so that they can be identified easily, and you'll move them to new positions.
2 In the Property inspector, in the CSS-P Element ID box, edit the text to read **Heatgraph**	To replace the default name that Dreamweaver assigned to the AP Div when it was created.
3 Click anywhere in the cayenne layer	(Layer is another name for AP Div.) The layer's border is highlighted, but the AP Div itself isn't selected—its content is. To modify the AP Div, you need to select it and not its contents.
Click the layer's selection handle, as shown	
	To select the AP Div itself and not its content.
4 Name this AP Div **Cayenne**	In the Property inspector, in the CSS-P Element box, edit the text to read Cayenne.
5 Drag the layer to the position shown on the heat graph	

6	Point to the lower-right resize handle	The pointer changes to a diagonal arrow, indicating that you can change the height and width of the layer simultaneously.
	Drag upwards and to the left, as shown	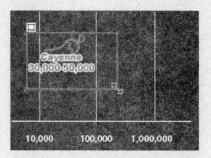
		To resize the layer so that it's only as large as it needs to be. This can make it easier to work with multiple layers.
7	Draw a new AP Div on the heat graph and name it **Habanero**	Click the Draw AP Div button, then drag to create the layer. In the Property inspector in the CSS-P Element box, name the layer Habanero.
	Insert habanero.gif into the Habanero layer	The image is in the heatgraph_images folder, in the images folder. Give the image the alternate text "Habanero."
8	Position the Habanero layer as shown	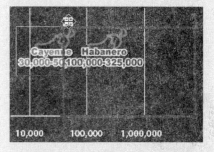
		(Drag from the layer's selection handle.) The pepper in the image should mark the heat rating on the chart. Because these will ultimately be pop-up images that appear one at a time, it's okay that they overlap.
	Resize the layer	So that it's only as large as it needs to be.
9	Create a new AP Div for the Chipotle image	Create a new AP Div and insert chipotle.gif into it.

10 Position the Chipotle layer as
    shown

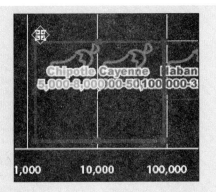

Resize the layer   So that it's only as large as it needs to be.

11 Save the document

Visibility

Explanation You can show or hide AP elements in Design view so that you can more easily position overlapping AP elements. By showing and hiding AP elements, you also can preview how a page will appear under various conditions.

To hide an AP element, activate the AP Elements panel, and click the eye icon so that it appears closed in the Visibility column, as shown in Exhibit 5-4. To show the AP element again, click the eye icon to open it.

To show and select an AP element in a document temporarily, click the AP element's name in the AP Elements panel. Clicking away from the AP element in the document hides the AP element again.

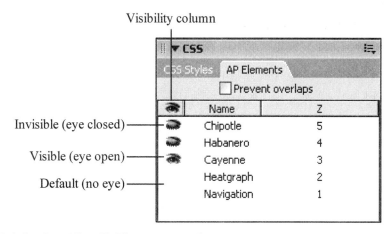

Exhibit 5-4: The AP Elements panel

Do it!

B-2: Setting visibility

Here's how	Here's why
1 Open the AP Elements panel	Activate AP Elements in the CSS panels group, or choose Window, AP Elements.
2 Click the Visibility column next to Chipotle, Habanero, and Cayenne	

CSS Styles	Layers	
☐ Prevent overlaps		
👁	Name	Z
👁	Chipotle	5
👁	Habanero	4
👁	Cayenne	3
	Heatgraph	2
	Navigation	1

To hide these three AP elements.

Save the page and preview it in Internet Explorer	To verify that the AP elements are not visible.
Close the browser	
3 In the AP Elements panel, select **Chipotle**	The AP Div becomes visible temporarily, but the eye icon shows that it wouldn't be visible in a browser.
In the Document window, click away from the AP Div	To deselect it. The AP Div is invisible again.
4 Save the document	Next, you'll assign behaviors to the AP Divs to control their visibility dynamically.

The Show-Hide Elements behavior

Explanation

With the Show-Hide Elements behavior, you can show, hide, or restore the default visibility of an element. You can use this behavior to control the visibility of an AP element dynamically. For example, you can have an AP Div appear when a user points to an object and disappear when the user points away from the object.

To control an element's visibility dynamically:

1   Select an object on the page to act as a rollover trigger.
2   Open the Behaviors panel, shown in Exhibit 5-5.
3   Click the Add behavior button and choose Show-Hide Elements.
4   From the Elements list, select the element you want to show, hide, or restore to default visibility.
5   Click Show, Hide, or Default.
6   Click OK.
7   In the Behaviors panel, click to the right of the event to activate the Event list.
8   Select the event to trigger the action from the Event list.

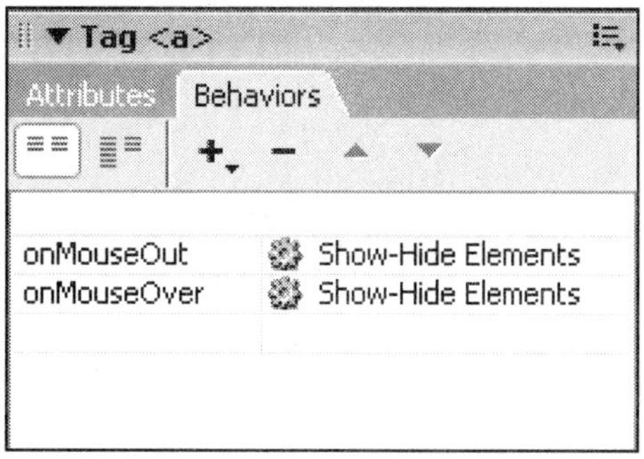

Exhibit 5-5: The Behaviors panel

Do it!

B-3:   Controlling visibility dynamically

Here's how	Here's why
1 In the navigation links layer, select the text **Cayenne**	You'll make this text act as a rollover trigger—the Cayenne layer will appear when a user points to it.
2 Open the Behaviors panel	(If necessary.) Activate the Behaviors tab in the Tag panel group, or choose Window, Behaviors.
3 Click the Add behavior button	
Choose **Show-Hide Elements**	To open the Show-Hide Elements dialog box.
4 In the Elements list, select **div "Cayenne"**	
Click **Show**	
Click **OK**	The action appears in the Behaviors panel. Notice that onClick is the default event to trigger the action. You'll change this to a different event handler.
5 From the Events list, select **onMouseOver**	
	To change the event handler for this behavior, so that the Cayenne layer appears when a user points to the text, "Cayenne." Next, you'll apply another behavior to make the layer disappear when the mouse isn't over the text.

6	Create a new Show-Hide Elements behavior	Click the Add behavior button and select Show-Hide Elements.
	Select **div "Cayenne"**	
	Click **Hide**	
	Click **OK**	
7	In the Behaviors panel, in the Events list, select **onMouseOut**	(The new action appears at the top of the list in the Behaviors panel.) To hide the layer when the pointer moves away from the text.
8	Save the page and preview it in Internet Explorer	Respond as necessary to security warnings.
9	Point to the Cayenne text	The Cayenne layer appears in the graph.
	Point away from the Cayenne text	The Cayenne layer disappears.
	Close the browser	
10	Select the text **Habanero**	You'll apply a Show-Hide Elements behavior to the Habanero layer.
	Apply a behavior to show the Habanero layer when a user points to the text	In the Behaviors panel, click the Add behavior button and select Show-Hide Elements. In the dialog box, select div "Habanero" and click Show. In the Behaviors panel, from the Events list, select onMouseOver.
	Apply a behavior to hide the Habanero layer when a user points away from the text	
11	Apply the same behaviors to the Chipotle layer	
12	Save the page and preview it in Internet Explorer	Respond as necessary to security warnings.
	Test the behaviors and close the browser	
13	Close the document	

Unit summary: AP elements

Topic A
In this topic, you learned how to insert **AP Divs**. You learned that any absolutely positioned element is an AP element that appears in the **AP Elements panel.** You learned how to insert an AP Div using the Draw AP Div tool, and you learned how to use **guides** to help you precisely position layers on a page.

Topic B
In this topic, you learned how to **select**, **name**, **resize**, and **position** AP Divs. You also learned how to control element **visibility** dynamically by applying the **Show-Hide Elements behavior.**

Independent practice activity

In this activity, you'll add new AP Divs to a page and insert images in them. Then you'll position the AP Divs and apply the Show-Hide Elements behavior to them.

1 Create a new site named **AP Div practice**, using the Outlander folder inside the Practice folder as the local root folder. (The Practice folder is located in the current unit folder.)

2 Open heatquiz.html.

3 Add an AP Div and insert **pepperonicini.gif** into it. Name the AP Div **Pepperonicini** and specify the same for the image's alternate text. (*Hint*: The image is in the heatgraph_images folder, in the images folder.)

4 Add an AP Div and insert **jalapeno.gif** into it. Make **Jalapeno** the AP Div's name and its alternate text.

5 Resize the AP Divs, so that they're only as large as they need to be to contain their images.

6 Position the new layers on the heat graph corresponding to their heat values, as shown in Exhibit 5-6.

7 In the navigation links layer, select the text **Pepperonicini**.

8 Apply a behavior to show the Pepperonicini layer when the user points to this text, and hide the layer when the user points away from the text.

9 Apply the same behavior to the Jalapeno text and its corresponding layer.

10 Hide all visible AP Divs, except the Heatgraph and Navigation layers.

11 Preview the page in Internet Explorer and test the behaviors.

12 Close the browser.

13 Close heatquiz.html.

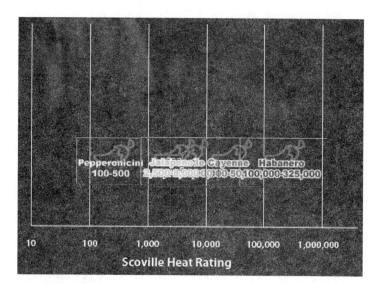

Exhibit 5-6: The position of the AP Div after step 6

Review questions

1 When you insert an AP Div using the Draw AP Div button, what tag does Dreamweaver use?

A The `<layer>` tag

B The `<div>` tag

C The `<divLayer>` tag

D The `<table>` tag

2 How can you select an AP Div and not its content? (Choose all that apply.)

A Click the AP Div's selection handle.

B Click anywhere inside the AP Div.

C Click the AP Div's border.

D In the AP Elements panel, click the AP Div's name.

3 To move an AP Div, you can: (Choose all that apply.)

A Drag its selection handle.

B Select its contents and drag.

C Press an arrow key to move the AP Div one pixel at a time.

D Hold down Shift and press an arrow key to move the AP Div one grid increment at a time.

4 How can you add a horizontal guide to a page?

   A Choose Insert, Guide, Horizontal, then drag the guide where you want it on the page.

   B Drag from the horizontal ruler to the location where you want the guide.

   C In the Document toolbar, from the Guide list, choose Horizontal, then drag the guide where you want it on the page.

   D Right-click the page and choose Insert, Guide, Horizontal, then drag the guide where you want it on the page.

5 To make an AP Div visible and invisible based on a user's action, you need to:

   A Set the AP Div to visible in the AP Elements panel.

   B Set the AP Div to invisible in the Layers palette.

   C Apply the Show-Hide Elements behavior to a trigger object.

   D Apply the Show-Hide Elements behavior to the AP Div itself.

6 To make an AP Div appear when a user clicks an object and then disappear when the pointer moves off the object, which event handlers should you use?

   A onMouseOver and onMouseOut, respectively.

   B onClick and onMouseDown, respectively.

   C onClick and onMouseOut, respectively.

   D onMouseUp and onMouseMove, respectively.

7 True or false? Setting an AP Div to visible or invisible in the AP Elements panel affects the AP Div only when viewed in Dreamweaver, not when viewed in a browser.

Unit 6

Multimedia

Unit time: 45 minutes

Complete this unit, and you'll know how to:

A Insert Flash buttons and Flash text.

B Add Flash and FlashPaper files to a Web page and add Windows Media Player files and QuickTime files.

C Create basic animation using the Timelines panel.

Topic A: Flash elements

This topic covers the following Adobe ACE exam objective for Dreamweaver CS3.

#	Objective
3.15	Add Flash elements to a page.

Using Flash elements

Explanation

You can make your Web pages more interactive and appealing by using Flash elements. Flash elements include:

- Flash buttons: small Flash files that act like rollover buttons: their appearances change in response to user actions.
- Flash text objects: small Flash files that contain text.

There are several advantages to using Flash objects instead of rollover buttons or GIF image-based text. These include:

- Flash objects are vector-based graphics, instead of raster graphics, such as JPEG and GIF files. If you resize a Flash object, it scales smoothly, instead of pixelating or distorting as a raster image does.
- A Flash button consists of a single file, rather than the multiple image files that a standard rollover button requires.

Flash buttons

A Flash button is a SWF file (a Flash movie) consisting of only four frames. The first three frames define the button states, which correspond to the link, hover (rollover), and active states of an HTML link. The fourth frame of the movie defines the hotspot for the button image. You can create Flash buttons by using Adobe Flash, or you can select from more than 40 pre-made Flash buttons that are included in Dreamweaver.

To add a Flash button to a page:

1 Place the insertion point on the page. Activate the Common tab on the Insert bar, click the Media list, and select Flash Button. (If the Flash Button is already active on the Insert bar, you can click it or drag it to the page.) The Insert Flash Button dialog box opens, as shown in Exhibit 6-1.

2 Select a style from the Style box.

3 In the Button text box, enter the text to appear on the button.

4 Select a font and enter a text size. The button is automatically sized to accommodate the text.

5 Define a link and a target type.

6 Save the button as a SWF file in the media or images folder of your Web site, depending on how you've structured your site folders.

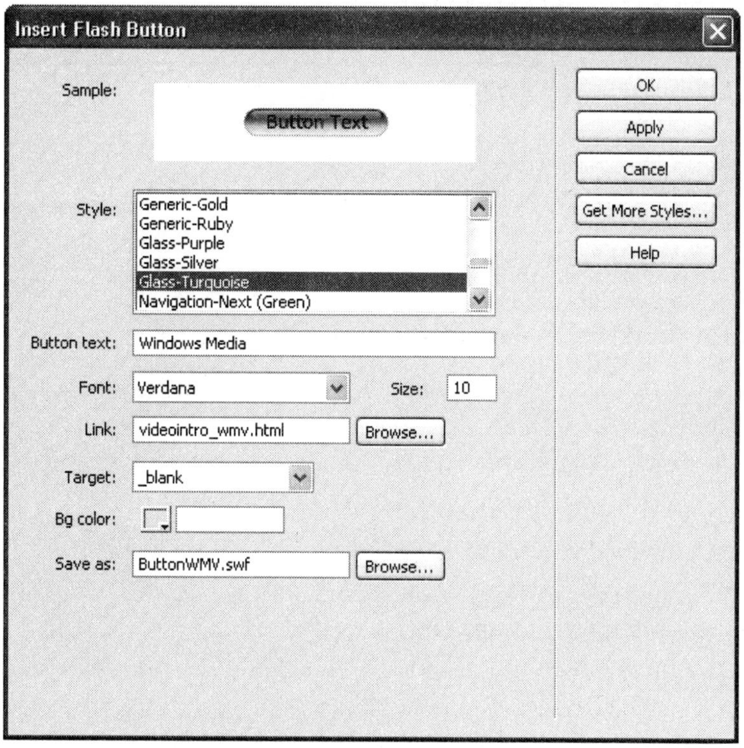

Exhibit 6-1: The Insert Flash Button dialog box

Do it!

A-1:   Inserting a Flash button

Here's how	Here's why
1 Choose **Site, New Site...**	
2 On the Advanced tab, name the site **Outlander media**	
In the Local root folder box, open and select the Outlander folder	(In the current unit folder.) Click the folder icon. Open the Outlander folder, and click Select.
Click **OK**	To create the site. Dreamweaver displays the site in the Files panel.
3 Open videos.html	You'll add Flash buttons that link two different video format previews.
4 Place the insertion point as shown	View the introdu |
5 Activate the Common tab on the Insert bar	
Click as shown	Flash Flash Button Flash Text FlashPaper Flash Video Shockwave Applet
	To display the media options.
Choose **Flash Button**	To open the Insert Flash Button dialog box.
6 Click **Apply**	To insert the button without closing the dialog box. Notice that the button is currently blank. You'll add text and functionality to the button.
7 From the Style list, select **Glass-Turquoise**	Scroll down the list.
In the Button text box, enter **Windows Media**	
In the Size box, enter **10**	

8 Next to the Link box, click **Browse**	You'll link the button to a page that contains a Windows Media file.
Select **videointro_wmv.html**	
Click **OK**	
9 From the Target list, select **_blank**	To set the link to open in a new browser window.
10 Edit the Save as box to read **ButtonWMV.swf**	
Click **Apply**	To preview the button on the page and confirm the settings.
Click **OK**	To close the Insert Flash Button dialog box. The Flash Accessibility Attributes dialog box appears. It's important to enter appropriate alternate text, just as with images, to ensure that the content or description of the content, depending on the context, is accessible to all browsers and other devices.
In the Title box, enter **Windows Media video button**	
Click **OK**	To close the dialog box.
11 Click to the right of the button	
	To place the insertion point.
12 On the Insert bar, click	To open the Insert Flash Button dialog box. You'll insert another Flash button.
Set the Style of the button to **Glass-Turquoise**	In the Style list, scroll down and select Glass-Turquoise.
Make the button text read **QuickTime**	
Set the button text size to **10**	
Link the button to **videointro_qt.html**	Next to the Link box, click Browse and select the file.
Set the link to open in a new window	From the Target list, select _blank.

13 Save the button as
    ButtonQT.swf

    Click **OK**   To close the dialog box. The Flash Accessibility
                                        Attributes dialog box appears.

    In the Title box, enter
    QuickTime video button

    Click **OK**

14 Click the Windows Media button   To select it. You'll preview the button in
                                        Dreamweaver.

    In the Property inspector, click   Expand the Property inspector, if necessary.
    Play

    Point to the **Windows Media**
    button

                                        To preview it. The button brightens gradually.

    In the Property inspector, click   To make the button editable.
    Stop

15 Save the page   The Copy Dependent Files dialog box appears.
                                        The buttons require a supporting javascript file,
                                        and Dreamweaver has copied it to your site
                                        folder. The dialog box reminds you to copy this
                                        file to your Web server when you upload the
                                        site.

    Click **OK**

16 Preview the page in Internet   Respond as necessary to security warnings.
    Explorer

17 Point to the buttons

    Click either button   The target page opens in a new window.

    Close both browser windows

Flash text

Explanation

A Flash text object is a small SWF file (a Flash movie). You can use Flash text objects to apply special fonts that your users might not have installed on their computers, and you can also apply a variety of special effects that aren't available with standard font sets.

You can create a simple Flash text object directly in Dreamweaver and save it as an SWF file. If you want to add or modify effects, you can edit the file in Adobe Flash.

To add a Flash text object to a page:

1 Place the insertion point on the page. On the Common tab of the Insert bar, click the Media list and select Flash Text. (If the Flash Text button already appears on the Insert bar, you can click it or drag it to the page.) The Insert Flash Text dialog box opens, as shown in Exhibit 6-2.

2 Format the text by using the controls at the top of the dialog box.

3 In the Text box, enter the text that you want to display.

4 Define a link and a target type.

5 Save the Flash text as an SWF file in an appropriate folder in your site structure.

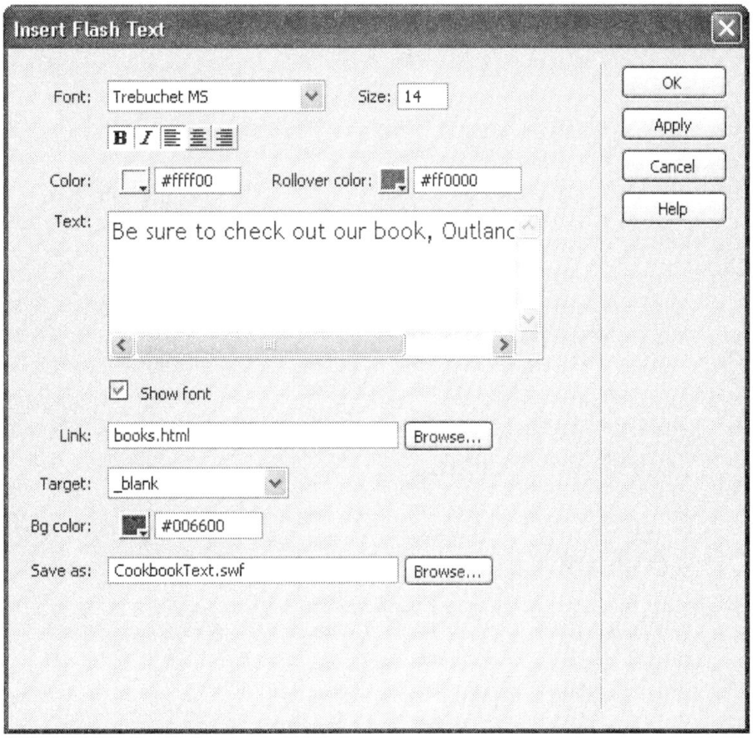

Exhibit 6-2: The Insert Flash Text dialog box

Do it!   **A-2: Inserting Flash text**

Here's how	Here's why
1 Click as shown	
	To place the insertion point next to the second button. You'll insert a Flash text object below the Flash buttons.
Press (← ENTER)	
2 From the Media: Flash Button list, choose **Flash Text**	(On the Insert bar.) To open the Insert Flash Text dialog box.
From the Font list, select **Trebuchet MS**	Scroll down.
Make the text bold and italic	Click the bold and italic buttons.
Set the font size to **24**	In the Size box, enter 24.
3 In the Color box, select the white color swatch	(In the leftmost column in the color picker.) The value should read #FFFFFF.
In the Rollover color box, select the yellow color swatch	(In the leftmost column in the color picker.) The value should read #FFFF00.
4 In the Text box, enter **Check out our book, "Outlander Cooking!"**	
5 In the Bg color box, enter **#006600**	This is the hexadecimal code for a shade of green.
Click **Apply**	To preview the Flash text.
6 Next to the Link box, click **Browse**	You'll link the Flash text to another page.
Select **books.html**	
Click **OK**	To add the path to the Link box.
In the Target list, select **_blank**	
7 Edit the Save as box to read **CookbookText.swf**	

8	Click **OK**	To close the dialog box. The Flash Accessibility Attributes dialog box appears.
	In the Title box, enter **Cookbook link**	
	Click **OK**	
9	In the Property inspector, click **Play**	To preview the Flash text.
	Point to the Flash text	To preview the rollover effect.
	In the Property inspector, click **Stop**	
10	In the Property inspector, click **Edit**	To open the Insert Flash Text dialog box. You'll reduce the font size.
	Change the font size to **14**	
	Click **OK**	
11	Save the page and preview it in Internet Explorer	
	Point to the Flash text	To verify that the rollover effect works.
	Click the Flash text	The books.html page opens.
	Close the browser windows	

Topic B: Multimedia content

This topic covers the following Adobe ACE exam objective for Dreamweaver CS3.

#	Objective
3.15	Add Flash elements to a page.

Flash content

Explanation

Dreamweaver makes it easy to add images, sound, video, and animation to your Web pages, so that you can deliver content in ways that static text alone can't.

You can add Flash content to a page by dragging the Flash button to the page. You can then use the Property inspector to define the size of the file as it appears on the page, adjust the video quality, set the animation to play automatically when the page loads, set it to play in a continuous loop, and apply styles to it.

To insert a Flash file:

1   Place the insertion point on the page. On the Common tab on the Insert bar, click the Media list and select Flash. (If the Flash button already appears on the Insert bar, you can click it or drag it to the page.) The Select File dialog box opens.

2   Select a Flash file and click OK.

3   In the Property inspector, edit the properties for the file.

Do it!   **B-1:   Inserting Flash content**

Here's how	Here's why
1 On the videos page, place the insertion point as shown	
	You'll insert a Flash file here.
2 On the Insert bar, from the Media: Flash Text list, choose **Flash**	The Select File dialog box appears.
Open the media subfolder	
Select **videopromo.swf**	
Click **OK**	The Object Tag Accessibility Attributes dialog box appears.
3 In the Title box, enter **Cooking video promo (Flash)**	
Click **OK**	
4 In the Property inspector, click **Play**	To preview the Flash file.
Click **Stop**	(In the Property inspector.) To make the Flash object editable.
5 Save the page and preview it in Internet Explorer	
After the Flash object has finished playing, close the browser	
6 Close videos.html	

FlashPaper

Explanation

You can use FlashPaper to embed a standard word processing document or other document type into a Web page. The document is presented to the user in its original format and layout, as shown in Exhibit 6-3. Users can use the tool bar at the top of the FlashPaper viewer to navigate between multiple pages, search the document content, zoom in and out, and print to a local printer.

FlashPaper files are created from a PDF version of the original document using Adobe FlashPaper 2. The FlashPaper file uses the SWF format developed for Flash files.

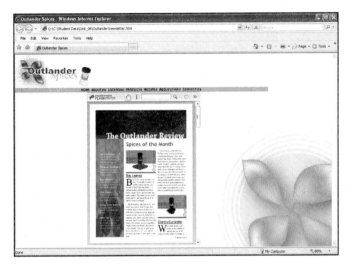

Exhibit 6-3: A standard 8½ inch by 11 inch document embedded as FlashPaper

After you insert a Flashpaper file, you can resize the object as needed. If you maintain the same height and width proportions, a whole page is viewable, instead of a portion of a page.

To insert a FlashPaper file:

1   Place the insertion point on the page. On the Common tab of the Insert bar, click the Media list and select FlashPaper. (If the FlashPaper button already appears on the Insert bar, you can click it or drag it to the page.) The Insert FlashPaper dialog box opens.

2   Next to the Source box, click the Browse button. The Select File dialog box opens.

3   Select a FlashPaper file and click OK.

4   Click OK

5   In the Document window, point to the object's lower-right corner handle. The pointer changes to a diagonal, double-sided arrow.

6   Press and hold Shift while dragging the handle to expand or reduce the size of the object. Doing so maintains the object's height and width proportions.

7   In the Property inspector, edit other properties as needed.

Do it!   **B-2:   Inserting a FlashPaper document**

Here's how	Here's why
1 Open newsletter.html	You'll insert an existing FlashPaper document that was created from a newsletter.
2 Double-click the text **Content**	To select it. You'll insert a FlashPaper file here.
On the Insert bar, from the Media list, choose **FlashPaper**	To open the Insert FlashPaper dialog box.
3 Next to Source, click **Browse**	To open the Select File dialog box.
Verify that the media subfolder is selected	In the Look in list.
Select **newsletter.swf**	
Click **OK**	To close the Select File dialog box.
4 In the Height box, enter **940**	In the Insert Flashpaper dialog box.
In the Width box, enter **725**	These values are proportional height and width measurements (8.5 x 11 inches is roughly proportional to 725 x 940 pixels).
Click **OK**	The Object Tag Accessibility Attributes dialog box appears.
5 In the Title box, enter **Outlander newsletter**	
Click **OK**	
6 Preview the FlashPaper object in Dreamweaver	(In the Property inspector, click Play.) The page is too large to fit into most browsers. You'll reduce its size so that more of the page is visible without scrolling.
Make the FlashPaper object editable	In the Property inspector, click Stop.
7 Scroll to the bottom of the Document window	You'll drag the FlashPaper object to resize it.

8 Click the FlashPaper object

(If necessary.) To select it.

Point as shown

(The lower-right corner of the FlashPaper object.) The pointer changes to a diagonal, double-sided arrow.

Press and hold (SHIFT)

Drag up and to the left until the width is about 450 pixels

To resize the object proportionally. The object's dimensions change in the Property inspector as you drag. You'll also center the object in the box.

9 Click to the right of the object

To place the insertion point.

In the Property inspector, click the Align Center button

To center the object.

10 Save the page and preview it in Internet Explorer

Respond as necessary to security warnings.

Click as shown

To navigate through the pages of the newsletter.

Navigate back to the first page

11 In the text box at the top of the FlashPaper, type **coriander**

You'll search the FlashPaper file for all references to this word.

Press (↵ ENTER)

The first match is highlighted.

Press (↵ ENTER)

To find the next instance of the word.

Close the browser

12 Close newsletter.html

Windows Media Player movies

Explanation   Windows Media Player is a popular video format for delivering multimedia content on Web pages. This format provides the user with a set of VCR-like playback controls.

To insert a Windows Media Player file:

1   Place the insertion point on the page. On the Common tab of the Insert bar, click the Media list and select Plugin. (If the Plugin button already appears on the Insert bar, you can click it or drag it to the page.) The Select File dialog box opens.

2   Select a WMV file and click OK.

3   In the Property inspector, edit the file's properties as needed.

Windows media file sizing

The developer of the movie file should provide you with the optimum viewing dimensions for this file in pixels. If this information isn't provided, you can use trial and error to arrive at a workable size and appropriate proportions. If the dimensions are provided, you need to add 64 pixels to the height to accommodate the playback controls at the bottom of the object.

B-3: Inserting a Windows Media Player movie

Here's how	Here's why
1 Open videointro_wmv.html	
2 Click as shown	
	You'll insert a Windows Media Player movie here.
3 On the Insert bar, from the Media list, choose **Plugin**	To open the Select File dialog box.
Select **cookingvideo.wmv**	From the media folder.
Click **OK**	
4 In the Property inspector, in the W box, enter **320**	To set the width of the video to 320 pixels.
5 Set the height to **304**	In the Property inspector, in the H box, enter 304 and press Enter. The actual height of the video is 240 pixels, but you need to add another 64 pixels to accommodate the user controls at the bottom of the movie.
6 Click to the right of the placeholder	To place the insertion point.
In the Property inspector, click the Align Center button	To center the object.
7 Save the page and preview it in Internet Explorer	
Point to the Windows Media Player controls	Tool tips describe the function of each control.
8 Click the Pause button	
Click the Play button	
When the movie ends, close the browser window	
9 Close videointro_wmv.html	

QuickTime movies

Explanation

The QuickTime movie format was originally developed for Macintosh computers, but a QuickTime plug-in is now installed on most Windows computers. If not, users can download it free of charge at www.apple.com/quicktime. Like the Windows Media Player, QuickTime provides playback controls for the user.

To insert a QuickTime movie:

1   Place the insertion point on the page. On the Common tab of the Insert bar, click the Media list and select Plugin. (If the Plugin button already appears on the Insert bar, you can click it or drag it to the page.) The Select File dialog box opens.

2   Select the MOV file and click OK.

3   In the Property inspector, edit the file's properties as needed.

QuickTime movie sizing

The developer of the QuickTime movie file should provide you with the optimum viewing dimensions for the file, in pixels. You need to add 20 pixels to a QuickTime object's height to accommodate the playback controls at the bottom of the object.

B-4:   Inserting a QuickTime movie

Here's how	Here's why
1 Open videointro_qt.html	You'll insert a QuickTime movie.
2 Drag the Plugin button to the indicated position	
	(From the Insert bar.) The Select File dialog box opens.
Select **cookingvideo.mov**	From the media folder.
Click **OK**	
3 Set the width to **320**	In the Property inspector, in the W box, enter 320.
4 Set the height to **260**	(In the Property inspector, in the H box, enter 260.) The actual height of the video is 240 pixels, but you need to add additional space to accommodate the user controls at the bottom of the movie.
5 Center the placeholder	Click to place the insertion point to the right of the placeholder, then click the Align Center button in the Property inspector.
6 Save the page and preview it in Internet Explorer	The movie begins to play automatically when the page finishes loading.
Test the user controls	
Close the browser	
7 Close videointro_qt.html	

Topic C: Timelines

Explanation

For most animation, it's best to use animation software, such as Flash. But you can create simple animation directly in Dreamweaver using AP elements and timelines. You can animate both images and AP elements along a timeline animation path.

Create a timeline

To create timeline animation using AP elements:

1 Select the AP element you want to animate, and then choose Modify, Timeline, Add Object to Timeline. The Timelines panel appears, as shown in Exhibit 6-4, and an animation bar representing the AP element is visible.

2 In the Timeline box, enter a descriptive name for the timeline.

3 Select the keyframe at the beginning of the animation bar, then position the AP element where you want the animation to begin. You can either drag it to position it, or enter values in the L (left) or T (top) boxes in the Property inspector.

4 Select the keyframe at the end of the animation bar, then position the AP element where you want the animation to end.

5 If you want the animation to begin playing when the page initially loads in a browser, check Autoplay.

6 If you want the animation to loop continuously, check Loop.

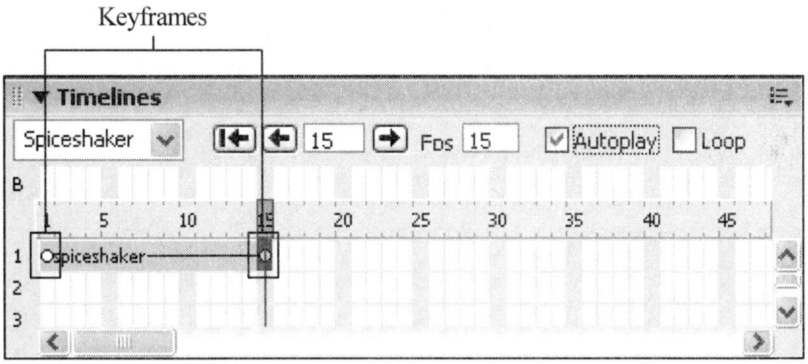

Exhibit 6-4: The Timelines panel

FPS (frames per second)

By default, timeline animations are set to 15 FPS (frames per second). This means that, for every second in the animation, you see 15 frames. Sometimes the FPS setting can make the animation look choppy. To increase the smoothness of animation, enter a larger value in the FPS box in the Timelines panel. In general, you want to stay between 15-30 FPS.

C-1: Creating a timeline animation

Here's how	Here's why
1 Open recipes.html	
2 Activate the AP Elements panel	If necessary.
Click each of the AP Elements in the panel	To view the corresponding div tags on the page. You'll use a timeline to animate the spice shaker, so that it slides in from the top of the page.
3 Select the spiceshaker div	
4 Choose **Window, Timelines**	To open the Timelines panel. A blank timeline is visible. You'll use this timeline to animate the spiceshaker div.
5 In the Timeline panel, in the name box, enter **Spiceshaker**	To name the timeline. To associate the timeline with the spiceshaker div, you need to add it to the timeline.
6 Choose **Modify, Timeline, Add Object to Timeline**	A dialog box appears, indicating the type of attributes Dreamweaver can animate for the selected div.
Click **OK**	To close the dialog box. The timeline now spans 15 frames. Also the FPS box is set to 15, indicating that the animation currently spans one second.
7 In the Property inspector, in the T box, type **–120px**	
Press ⏎ ENTER	This positions the div so that just the bottom of it is visible at the top of the page. This is where you want the div to be when the animation begins.

8	In the Timelines panel, click the keyframe at the end of the bar	
		To select it. You'll position the spiceshaker div where you want it to be when the animation ends.
	In the Property inspector, in the T box, enter **0px**	(Type 0px in the T box, and press Enter.) Doing so positions the div back in its original position. This is where you want the div to be when the animation ends. You'll set the animation to play when the page first loads in a browser.
9	Check **Autoplay**	(In the Timelines panel.) A dialog box appears, indicating that Dreamweaver is automatically adding the Play Timeline action using an onLoad event to trigger the animation to begin when the page loads.
	Click **OK**	To close the dialog box.
10	Save the page and preview it in Internet Explorer	(Respond as necessary to security warnings.) When the page loads, the spice shaker drops in from the top of the page.
	Click the Refresh button	To view the animation more than once. The animation is a little choppy. You'll adjust the frame rate to make it smoother.
	Close the browser	To return to Dreamweaver.
11	In the Timelines panel, in the FPS box, enter **30**	
		To increase the frame rate to 30 frames per second.
12	Save the page and preview it in Internet Explorer	The animation plays more smoothly. (Click the Refresh button to replay the animation, if necessary.)
13	Close the browser, and close recipes.html	
14	Right-click the Timelines panel	
	Choose **Close Panel Group**	To close the Timelines panel.

Unit summary: Multimedia

Topic A   In this topic, you learned that you can make your pages more interactive and appealing by using Flash elements. You learned how to add **Flash buttons** and **Flash text** to a Web page, and you learned how to modify the appearance of Flash text.

Topic B   In this topic, you learned how to add **Flash** files and **FlashPaper** files to a page. You learned that you can use FlashPaper to embed word processing documents or other document types in a Web page and retain the document's original formatting. You also learned how to insert **Windows Media Player** files and **QuickTime** files.

Topic C   In this topic, you learned how to create **basic animation** by creating and manipulating a **timeline** in the Timelines panel.

Independent practice activity

In this activity, you'll insert a Flash file and a Flash button. You'll format the Flash button and then test the Flash content in your browser.

1 Create a new site named **Media practice**, using the Outlander folder inside the Practice folder as the local root folder. (The Practice folder is in the current unit folder.)

2 Open books.html.

3 At the top of the mainColumn div, insert the Flash file, **bookpromo.swf**. (The file is in the Practice\Outlander\media folder.)

4 At the bottom of the mainColumn div, insert a Flash button.

5 Select a style for the button, other than the default style. Be sure to use a button style that supports text (as opposed to one that shows just an arrow, for example).

6 Set the button text to read **Videos**.

7 Link the button to videos.html, which is located in the Practice\Outlander folder.

8 Preview the page in Internet Explorer.

9 Verify that the Flash file plays automatically when the page opens.

10 Verify that the Flash button works as expected.

11 Close the browser.

12 Close books.html.

Review questions

1 True or false? Flash objects are raster objects like GIF and JPEG files.

2 How can you preview a Flash animation in a page? (Choose all that apply.)

   A Double-click the Flash placeholder.

   B Update the page, then preview it in a browser.

   C Chooose View, Preview Flash.

   D In the Property inspector, click the Play/Stop button.

3 Advantages of using Flash text include: (Choose all that apply.)

   A It loads faster than plain HTML text.

   B You can use exotic fonts that users aren't likely to have installed on their computers.

   C You can apply special effects that aren't available with standard font sets.

   D Search engines can locate Flash text easier than plain HTML text.

4 How can you add a Flash button to a page?

   A In the Common category of the Insert bar, click the Media list and select Flash Button.

   B Choose Insert, Image Objects, Rollover image.

   C In the Behaviors panel, click the Add behavior button and select Add Flash Button.

   D Drag the Flash button from the Files panel to the page.

5 Advantages of using FlashPaper include: (Choose all that apply.)

   A You can embed files, such as PDFs and Word documents, into a Web page.

   B You can send and receive information from your users.

   C Documents are presented in their original format and layout.

   D Users can search the document, print it, and zoom in and out as needed.

6 When you insert a QuickTime movie, how many pixels should you add to the object's height to accommodate the playback controls at the bottom of the object?

   A 30

   B 50

   C 64

   D 20

7 When you insert a Windows Media Player file, how many pixels should you add to the object's height to accommodate the playback controls at the bottom of the object?

A 30

B 50

C 64

D 20

8 When working with timeline animation, how can you define the position of an AP div tag at the end of the animation? (Choose all that apply.)

A Position the AP div tag where you want it when the animation ends, then right-click it and choose End Animation.

B In the Timelines panel, select the keyframe at the end of the animation bar, then select the AP div tag and enter positioning values in the L and T boxes.

C Position the AP div tag where you want it when the animation ends, then right-click the timeline in the Timelines panel and choose End Animation.

D In the Timelines panel, select the keyframe at the end of the animation bar, then drag to position the AP div tag where you want the animation to end.

Unit 7

Working with XML

Unit time: 60 minutes

Complete this unit, and you'll know how to:

A Convert an HTML page to an XSLT file and bind XML data to an XSLT file.

B Create a repeat region in an XSLT file, create dynamic links, and attach an XSLT page to an XML document.

Topic A: XML and XSLT

This topic covers the following Adobe ACE exam objective for Dreamweaver CS3.

#	Objective
3.16	List and describe the functionality provided by Dreamweaver for XML.

XML

Explanation

XML (Extensible Markup Language) is a structured language that organizes document components as data, so you can reuse the content in a variety of formats. It's similar to HTML in that it uses markup tags to organize and display content. However, instead of relying on a standard set of markup tags, XML allows you to create your own elements based on what makes sense for your content, as illustrated in Exhibit 7-1. You can then specify what happens to the labeled content in terms of what's published, how it's presented, and so forth. XML documents are just text documents. The elements within an XML document simply provide a structure for the content from which you can draw.

XML elements

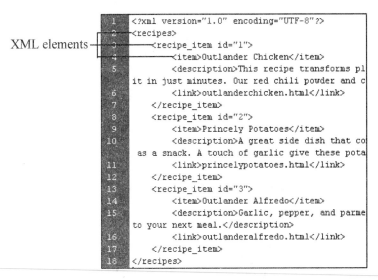

```
1   <?xml version="1.0" encoding="UTF-8"?>
2   <recipes>
3       <recipe_item id="1">
4           <item>Outlander Chicken</item>
5           <description>This recipe transforms pl
    it in just minutes. Our red chili powder and c
6           <link>outlanderchicken.html</link>
7       </recipe_item>
8       <recipe_item id="2">
9           <item>Princely Potatoes</item>
10          <description>A great side dish that co
    as a snack. A touch of garlic give these pota
11          <link>princelypotatoes.html</link>
12      </recipe_item>
13      <recipe_item id="3">
14          <item>Outlander Alfredo</item>
15          <description>Garlic, pepper, and parme
    to your next meal.</description>
16          <link>outlanderalfredo.html</link>
17      </recipe_item>
18  </recipes>
```

Exhibit 7-1: An example of an XML document

XSL and XSLT

To organize XML data in a way that makes sense in a browser, you need to format it using XSL (Extensible Stylesheet Language). XSL allows you to format XML data much the same way that CSS allows you to format HTML content. You can generate styles in the XSL file, and then attach it to the XML file so that, when users access the XML page, it looks the way you defined it in the XSL styles.

XSLT (Extensible Stylesheet Language Transformations) is a subset of XSL that lets you display XML data in a browser by transforming it into HTML. You can create XSLT pages in Dreamweaver and then use them like templates to control page layout and other design attributes.

With XSLT, you can create client-side transformations or server-side transformations. When you perform a server-side transformation, the server does the work of transforming the XML and XSL, while a client-side transformation requires that a browser do the work. Both methods offer advantages and disadvantages, which are described in the following table.

Method	Advantages	Disadvantages
Client-side transformations	Server configuration is simpler. The server can respond to requests quickly, because the processing burden is pushed to the client.	Not all browsers are capable of executing an XSLT transformation. (Although most current browsers, such as Explorer 6+, Netscape 8, and Firefox 1.0.2+ all support XSLT.) Privacy issues may be involved in delivering your XML to the client.
Server-side transformations	No browser versioning issues. Only HTML is delivered from the server, and all data are kept private.	Requires integration with a programming language to execute correctly, which increases the complexity of the server configuration.

Convert HTML pages to XSLT pages

Although you can create XSLT pages from scratch, it's generally easier to convert an existing HTML page to XSLT, and then add the XML components. To convert an HTML page, open the page, then choose File, Convert, XSLT 1.0. Dreamweaver creates a new XSLT page, based on the original HTML page, and automatically saves it to the current site folder.

Do it!

A-1: Converting an HTML page to an XSLT page

Here's how	Here's why
1 Choose **Site**, **New Site...**	
2 On the Advanced tab, name the site **Outlander XML**	
In the Local root folder box, open and select the Outlander folder	(In the current unit folder.) Click the folder icon. Open the Outlander folder, and click Select.
Click **OK**	To create the site. Dreamweaver displays the site in the Files panel.
3 Open recipes.html	(From the Files panel.) The page consists of a short description of one recipe. You want to add more recipes to the page, and you'll control the content using XML.
4 Open monthlyrecipes.xml	The XML document contains content for three recipes. The content for each recipe is divided into \<item\>, \<description\>, and \<link\> elements.
5 Activate recipes.html	You'll use this HTML page to create an XSLT page for the XML.
6 Choose **File**, **Convert**, **XSLT 1.0**	A new XSLT page titled "recipes.xsl" is created and is automatically saved within the site.
In the Files panel, click the Refresh button	(If necessary.) To refresh the file listing. The new page is visible. You'll work with this new XLST page instead of the original HTML page.
7 Close recipes.html	

Binding XML data

Explanation
For the purposes of this course, you'll execute a client-side transform. This means that you'll add XML data to an XLST page, and a browser will do the work of transforming the data into HTML. To add XML data to an XSLT page, you first need to reference the XML document within the Bindings panel.

To reference an XML document:

1   Choose Window, Bindings to open the Bindings panel, if necessary.

2   Click the Source link in the upper-right corner of the panel, or click the XML link that appears prior to linking to an XML document.

3   In the Locate XML Source dialog box, verify that Attach a local file on my computer or local area network option is selected. (If you're executing a server-side transform, you select the Attach a remote file on the Internet option.)

4   Click Browse to open the Locate Source XML for XSL Template dialog box.

5   Navigate to the location of the XML document to which you want to link, then select the document, and click OK.

6   Click OK to reference the XML document in the Bindings panel. The schema for the XML document appears as a hierarchy, as shown in Exhibit 7-2.

Exhibit 7-2: The Bindings panel

Schema icons

The hierarchy of the schema shows a series of ◇ bracket icons that represent each element in the XML document. For example, in Exhibit 7-2, the "◇ description" element is a child element of the "◇ recipe_item" element. Some icons have additional identifiers, such as the small plus sign included with the ◇ recipe_item element. The following table describes the icons that may appear in the schema.

Icon	Description
◇	XML element – An element that appears only once within its parent element.
◇⁺	Repeating XML element – An element that appears more than once within its parent element.
◇?	Optional XML element – An element that appears within one or more repeating elements, but not in all repeating elements.
@	XML attribute

Adding XML elements to pages

After you reference an XML document, you can add the XML elements to the XSLT page by dragging them from the Bindings panel to the page. When you do so, Dreamweaver places XML data placeholders at the location you dragged, similar to the example shown in Exhibit 7-3. These placeholders are linked to the elements in the XML document. When you preview the page in a browser, the browser uses the placeholders to reference the XML content and displays it in the page.

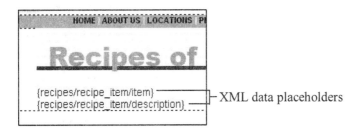

Exhibit 7-3: XML data placeholders in an XSLT page

Formatting XML data placeholders

You can use CSS to format XML data placeholders, similar to the way you format HTML content. Select the placeholder you want to format, and then select a style from the Style list in the Property inspector.

Do it!   **A-2:   Binding XML data to an XSLT page**

Here's how	Here's why
1 Activate the Bindings panel	(Choose Window, Bindings.) You'll bind XML data to the document.
2 In the Bindings panel, click the XML link, as shown	Database **Bindings** Server Be Componer XSLT (Entire page) Source.. C To use an XML reference in this XSLT page: 1. Please attach XML source document. To open the Locate XML Source dialog box.
3 Verify that **Attach a local file on my computer or local area network** is selected	
4 Click **Browse**	The Locate Source XML for XSL Template dialog box appears.
Select **monthlyrecipes.xml**, and click **OK**	

5 Click **OK**	Database **Bindings** Server Be Componer
	
	XSLT (Entire page) Source.. C
	
	⊟ 🖉 Schema for monthlyrecipes.xml
	  ⊟ ⟨⟩ recipes
	    ⊟ ⟨⟩⁺ recipe_item
	       @ id
	      ⟨⟩ item
	      ⟨⟩ description
	      ⟨⟩ link
	
	The schema for the monthlyrecipes.xml document is visible in the panel.

6 Select all of the recipe text on the page

(Don't select the Recipes of the Month graphic.) You'll remove this placeholder text and add XML placeholders to the page.

Press (DELETE)

The content you deleted had formatting applied to it that's still active. You'll remove the formatting before you add the placeholders.

In the Property inspector, from the Format list, select **Paragraph**

7 From the Bindings panel, drag the item element to the page, as shown

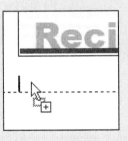

An XML data placeholder that corresponds to the recipe titles appears on the page . You want the recipe descriptions to be just below the titles.

8 Press the right arrow key

To place the insertion point to the right of the placeholder.

Press (SHIFT) + (↵ ENTER)

{recipes/recipe_item/item}

To add a line break.

9   Drag the description element below the item placeholder, as shown

{recipes/recipe_item/item}
{recipes/recipe_item/description}

Drag the element from the Bindings panel.

10   Save the page and preview it in Internet Explorer

When you preview the page, the first recipe stored in the XML document is visible.

Close the browser

To return to Dreamweaver. You'll format the placeholders in order to format the corresponding XML content.

11   Click the description XML data placeholder

(If necessary.) To select it.

In the Property inspector, from the Style list, select **recipedescriptions**

| None |
| imageRight |
recipedescriptions
Rename...
Attach Style Sheet...

> \<p>

Style | None   ▼   CSS

Size | 90   ▼   %   ▼

To apply the style to the placeholder.

12   Click the item XML data placeholder

To select it.

In the Property inspector, click the Italic button

To italicize the text.

13   Save the page and preview it in Internet Explorer

The recipe uses the same formatting you applied to the placeholders.

Close the browser

To return to Dreamweaver.

Topic B: Manipulation of XML data

This topic covers the following Adobe ACE exam objective for Dreamweaver CS3.

#	Objective
3.16	List and describe the functionality provided by Dreamweaver for XML.

Repeat Regions

Explanation

After you add XML content to an XSLT page, you can manipulate the content in various ways. For example, you can create regions for XSLT documents that work like template regions, or you can generate dynamic links for XML data placeholders that direct viewers to other pages.

In some ways, XSLT pages are like template documents. They're linked to XML documents and provide the layout structure through which the XML data displays in a browser. Like templates, XSLT pages also include regions you can add to streamline the process of adding XML data. For example, if your XML document includes repeating elements, as shown in Exhibit 7-4, you can use a repeat region to instruct a browser to list content automatically within those elements without having to drag placeholders manually for each of them.

```
<?xml version="1.0" encoding="UTF-8"?>
<recipes>
    <recipe_item id="1">
        <item>Outlander Chicken</item>
        <description>This recipe transforms
it in just minutes. Our red chili powder and          — Repeating elements
        <link>outlanderchicken.html</link>
    </recipe_item>
    <recipe_item id="2">
        <item>Princely Potatoes</item>
        <description>A great side dish that
as a snack. A touch of garlic give these po
        <link>princelypotatoes.html</link>
    </recipe_item>
```

Exhibit 7-4: An example of repeating elements within an XML document

To add a repeat region:

1. Select the XML data placeholder(s) you want to include in the region.
2. On the Insert bar, activate the XSLT tab.
3. Click the Repeat Region icon to open the XPath Expression Builder dialog box, shown in Exhibit 7-5. You can also choose Insert, XSLT Objects, Repeat Region.
4. In the XML schema, select the repeating element you want to assign to the repeat region. Repeating elements appear with a small plus sign next to them.
5. Click OK. In the XSLT document, a thin, gray outline appears around the selected placeholders. Also, the length of the placeholders is shortened.

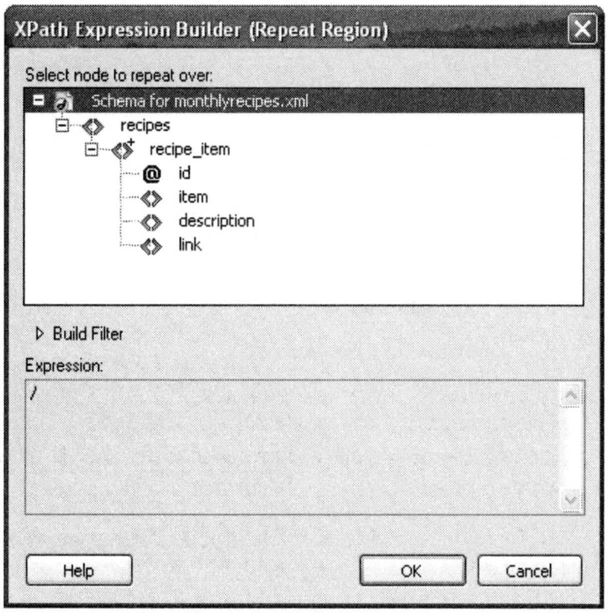

Exhibit 7-5: The XPath Expression Builder dialog box

In Dreamweaver, the repeat region shows only the original placeholders you established earlier. However, when you preview the page in a browser, each instance of the repeating element in the XML document is added.

B-1: Creating a repeat region

Here's how	Here's why
1 Shift-select the two XML placeholders	To select them both. You'll create a repeat region that instructs a browser to display the title and description for the remaining recipes in the XML document.
2 On the Insert bar, activate the XSLT tab	
Click [icon]	(The Repeat Region button.) To open the XPath Expression Builder dialog box.

3 Under Select node to repeat over, select the recipe_item element	Select node to repeat over:
	Schema for monthlyrecipes.xml
	  recipes
	    recipe_item
	      id
	      item

	Repeating elements are indicated by a small plus sign.
Click **OK**	A thin, tabbed, gray outline appears around the placeholders. Also, the length of the placeholders is shortened.
4 Save the page and preview it in Internet Explorer	Two additional recipes are now included in the XML document. However, there are no breaks between the recipes, and they run together in one paragraph.
Close the browser	To return to Dreamweaver. You'll add line breaks after the description placeholder to add space between the recipes.
5 Click the description placeholder	To select it.
Press the right arrow	To place the insertion point immediately to the right of the placeholder.
Press (↵ ENTER) twice	To add line breaks after the placeholder.
6 Save the page and preview it in Internet Explorer	The recipes are now spaced apart.
Close the browser	

Dynamic links

Explanation

You can create links for XML placeholders using the conventional method of specifying the file path for the link in the Property inspector. However, if the link resides within a repeating region, the same link is applied in each repetition. To circumvent this, you can automate the linking process by creating an element in the XML document specifically for link information, and then create a dynamic link to the element in the XSLT page. With this method, the link within the repeating region changes with each repeating element repetition.

To create dynamic links:

1 Select the XML data placeholder you want to use for the link.

2 In the Property inspector, to the right of the Link box, click the Browse for File icon.

3 In the Select File dialog box, next to Select file name from, select the Data sources option. The dialog box displays the XML schema for the referenced XML document, as shown in Exhibit 7-6.

4 Select the element in the schema that contains the link file path information.

5 Click OK to create the link.

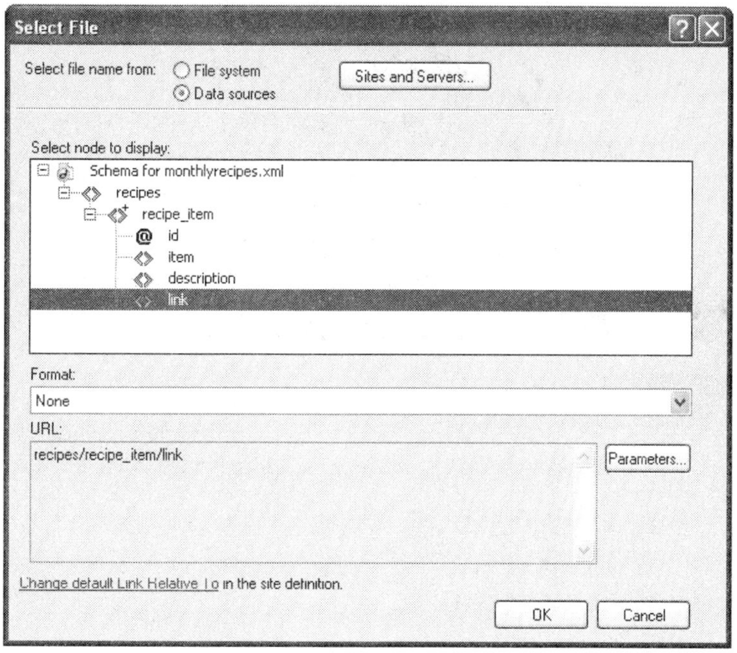

Exhibit 7-6: The Select File dialog box with data sources visible

B-2: Creating a dynamic link

Here's how	Here's why
1 Click the item placeholder	To select it. You'll create a dynamic link that directs viewers to the recipe directions when they click the recipe titles.
2 In the Property inspector, to the right of the Link box, click the Browse for File icon	
	To open the Select File dialog box.
3 Next to Select file name from, select **Data sources**	
4 Under Select node to display, select the link element	
Click **OK**	
5 Click a blank area of the page	The title placeholder uses the same formatting as the other page links, such as those in the navigation bar.
6 Save the page and preview it in Internet Explorer	
7 Point to each of the recipe titles	The titles are links and use the link formatting established in the CSS style sheet.
8 Click the Outlander Chicken link	The browser navigates to the page containing the Outlander Chicken recipe.
Click the Back button	To return to the recipes page.
9 Click the other recipe links	Each link dynamically directs users to the recipe directions.
Close the browser	

Attaching an XSLT page to an XML document

Explanation

Although you can preview the XSLT page in a browser, it's ultimately a template for the XML document, which is what users need to access after the site is uploaded to a remote server. To make the XSLT page work correctly on the server side, you need to attach it to the XML document.

To attach an XSLT page to an XML document:

1 Open the XML document for which you want to attach the XSLT page.
2 Choose Commands, Attach an XSLT Stylesheet to open the Attach an XSLT Stylesheet dialog box.
3 Click Browse, then navigate to the location of the XSLT page, select it, and click OK.
4 Click OK to attach the page.

After you attached an XSLT page to an XML document, you can preview the XML document in a browser. When you do so, the browser uses the attached XSLT page to construct the layout of the page, similar to the way a CSS style sheet controls the layout and styles of HTML pages.

Updating XML content

An advantage of using XML is that you can update and change page content without having to work directly in the XSLT page. This can help control site integrity because other people who might not be familiar with the site design can update the content without the possibility of accidentally changing the layout. Also, because XML documents are text documents, changes can be made outside of Dreamweaver. After the changes are made in the XML document, you need only to upload the document to the server for the changes to take effect.

B-3: Attaching an XSLT page to an XML document

Here's how	Here's why
1 Activate monthlyrecipes.xml	To view the XML document containing the recipes content. You'll attach the XSLT page to this XML document.
2 Choose **Commands**, **Attach an XSLT Stylesheet**	To open the Attach an XSLT Stylesheet dialog box.
3 Click **Browse**	To open the Select XSLT File dialog box.
Select **recipes.xsl** and click **OK**	Be sure to select recipes.xsl, not recipes.html.

Click **OK**	`<?xml version="1.0" encoding="UTF-8"?>`
	`<?xml-stylesheet href="recipes.xsl" type="text/`
	`<recipes>`

	To close the Attach an XSLT Stylesheet dialog box. A reference link to the XSLT page appears at the top of the XML document.
4 Save the XML page and preview it in Internet Explorer	When you preview the XML document, it references the XSLT page you created earlier.
Close the browser	Now you can use the XML document to make content updates to the page without having to work within the XSLT layout.

5 Place the insertion point as shown	`<recipe_item id="3">`
	`    <item>Outlander Alfredo`
	`    <description>Garlic, pe`
	`your next meal.</description`
	`    <link>outlanderalfredo.`

	(At the beginning of the description text for the Outlander Alfredo recipe.) You'll add content here.
Type **Try this lighter version of a creamy classic.**	
6 Save the XML page and preview it in Internet Explorer	The additional content is visible in the Outlander Alfredo recipe description text.
7 Close the browser, and close all open documents	

Unit summary: Working with XML

Topic A   In this topic, you learned how to convert an **HTML** page to an **XSLT page**, so that you can incorporate content from an XML document. You also referenced the XML document in the **Bindings panel** and used the schema to add **XML placeholders** within the XSLT page.

Topic B   In this topic, you learned how to create **repeat regions** in an XSLT page, so that a browser can display all the repeating elements in an XML document. You also created **dynamic links** and attached an **XSLT page** to an **XML document**.

Independent practice activity

In this activity, you'll create a "top selling" products page and use XML to control the page content. You'll convert an existing HTML page to an XSLT page, and then use the elements in an XML document to determine the page content.

1   Create a new site named **XML practice**, using the Outlander folder inside the Practice subfolder as your local root folder. (*Hint*: Make sure you start with the current unit folder.)

2   Open products.html. Convert the HTML page to an XSLT page. (*Hint:* Choose File, Convert, XSLT 1.0.) Then, close the original HTML document.

3   In the Bindings panel, link the topsellers.xml document. (*Hint:* In the Bindings panel, click the XML link.)

4   Delete the cinnamon content in the left table cell. Remove any formatting applied to the text. Delete the price in the right table cell.

5   Drag the item element from the Bindings panel to the left table cell.

6   Drag the description element from the Bindings panel to the right of the item placeholder. Add a line break between the placeholders, similar to the example shown in Exhibit 7-7.

7   Drag the price element from the Bindings panel to the right table cell.

8   Save the page and preview it in Internet Explorer. When you're finished, close the browser.

9   Create a dynamic link for the item placeholder that references the link element in the XML document. (*Hint:* Select the item placeholder, then click the Browse for File icon in the Property inspector. Select Data sources, then select the link element in the schema, and click OK.)

10 In the Quick Tag Selector at the bottom of the document window, click the <tr> tag to select the entire table row. Create a repeat region for the selected row. (*Hint:* In the Insert bar's XSLT tab, click the Repeat Region icon. Select the product_item repeating element in the schema, then click **OK**.)

11 Save the page and preview it in Internet Explorer. Click some of the links to test them. When you're finished, close the browser.

12 Link the XSLT page to the XML document. (*Hint:* Open the topsellers.xml document, then choose Commands, Attach an XSLT Stylesheet. Navigate to the products.xsl page, select it, then click OK.)

13 Save the XML document and preview it in Internet Explorer. When you're finished, close the browser.

14 Close all open documents.

Exhibit 7-7: The item and description placeholders after step 6

Review questions

1 Which are advantages of client-side transformations? (Choose all that apply.)

A No browser versioning issues.

B Only HTML is delivered from the server, and all your data are kept private.

C The server can respond to requests quickly, because the processing burden is pushed to the client.

D Server configuration is simpler.

2 How can you convert an HTML page to an XSLT page?

A Choose Commands, Convert to XSLT 1.0.

B In the Files panel, right-click the page and choose rename, then change the file extension from .html to .xsl.

C Choose File, Convert, XSLT 1.0.

D Right-click anywhere on the page, then choose Convert to XSLT 1.0.

3 How can you reference an XML document in the Bindings panel? (Choose all that apply.)

A In the Files panel, right-click the XML document, then choose Bind to current page.

B Click the XML link in the panel, then navigate to the location of the XML document and click OK.

C Drag the XML document from the Files panel to the Bindings panel.

D Click the Source link in the upper-right corner of the panel, then navigate to the location of the XML document and click OK.

4 How can you add a repeat region to an XSLT page? (Choose all that apply.)

   A Choose Insert, XSLT Objects, Repeat Region.

   B From the Bindings panel, drag a repeating element icon to the page.

   C Right-click where you want to add the region, then choose Add Repeat Region.

   D In the Insert bar, under the XSLT category, click the Repeat Region icon.

5 How can you create a dynamic link for a selected XML placeholder?

   A Double-click the placeholder. Select the Data sources option, then select a repeating element from the XML schema and click OK.

   B In the Property inspector, click the Browse for File icon. Select the Data sources option, then select a repeating element from the XML schema, and click OK.

   C In the Property inspector, enter the file path for the link in the File box.

   D Double-click the placeholder, then the file path for the link in the File box, and click OK.

6 How can you attach an XSLT page to an XML document?

   A Open the XML document, then choose Commands, Attach an XSLT Stylesheet. Navigate to the location of the XSLT page, select it, then click OK.

   B In the File panel, right-click the XSLT page, then choose Link to XML. Navigate to the location of the XML document, select it, then click OK.

   C In the File panel, right-click the XML document, then choose Link to XSLT. Navigate to the location of the XSLT page, select it, then click OK.

   D Open the XLST page, then choose Commands, Attach an XML Document. Navigate to the location of the XML document, select it, then click OK.

Unit 8

Collaboration and publishing

Unit time: 30 minutes

Complete this unit, and you'll know how to:

A Use Check In/Check Out options and manage files in a group work setting.

B Check for browser-specific errors.

C Check for and fix accessibility problems.

Topic A: Collaboration

This topic covers the following Adobe ACE exam objectives for Dreamweaver CS3.

#	Objective
3.19	Annotate files by using Design Notes and Comments
4.1	Manage collaboration with multiple developers by using Check In – Check Out.

Check In/Check Out options

Explanation

If you're one of a group of people working on a site, the Check In/Check Out Files option provides a way to prevent more than one person at a time from working on a file. Dreamweaver uses an icon system next to filenames to help you keep track of your files and their check in/check out status.

When you check out a file (or files), Dreamweaver displays a green check mark next to the files, as shown in Exhibit 8-1. If another user checks out a file, Dreamweaver displays a red check mark next to the files. You can't edit files with a red check mark, until the person using them checks them back in. However, you can find information about the person using the files by right-clicking them and choosing Show Checked Out By.

When you check files back in, a lock icon appears next to them, indicating that they're read-only. You can't make further changes to the file until you check it out again.

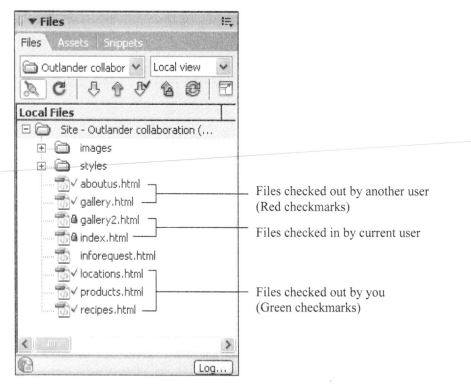

Exhibit 8-1: The Files panel with Check In/Check Out options enabled

To enable the Check In/Check Out system:

1 Choose Site, Manage Sites to open the Manage Sites dialog box.

2 Select the site, then click the Edit button to open the Site Definition dialog box.

3 Activate Advanced.

4 In the Category list, select Remote Info.

5 Check Enable file check in and check out.

6 If you want Dreamweaver to check out files automatically when you open them, check Check out files when opening.

7 Click OK.

To check files in or out manually:

1 In the Files panel, select the file(s) you want to check out.

2 Click the Check In or Check Out buttons at the top of the panel, as shown in Exhibit 8-2. If you opted to check out files automatically when you open them, open one of the files. When you check out a file, Dreamweaver replaces the local copy of the document with the remote copy.

3 Click Yes or No to include dependent files. If the local site is currently the same as the remote site, it isn't necessary to include dependent files.

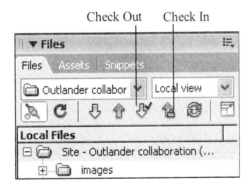

Exhibit 8-2: Check Out/Check In buttons in the Files panel

Sometimes you might decide you don't want to incorporate the changes you made after you've checked a file back in. You can undo the changes by opening the file and choosing Site, Undo Check Out.

Compare files

It isn't uncommon to have multiple versions of the same page in the site folder. For example, you might have various versions of a page for specific browsers, or you might have reworked the structure of a page and saved a copy of the original from which to grab the content. In the latter case, Dreamweaver can compare the two files for differences in content.

To compare files, you must install a third-party file comparison tool, which you can locate and download by performing a search on the Adobe site.

After you've installed the comparison tool, you can compare both local and remote files. To compare to local files, select both files in the Files panel, then right-click one of them and choose Compare local files. To compare two remote files, display the remote files by connecting to the server, then choose Compare Remote Files. To compare a local file with a remote file, right-click one of the files in the Files panel, then choose Compare with Remote.

A-1: Checking files in and out

Here's how	Here's why
1 Choose **Site, New Site…**	
2 On the Advanced tab, name the site **Collaboration**	
In the Local root folder box, open and select the Outlander folder	(In the current unit folder.) You'll configure a local folder as the "remote" site and enable Check In/Check Out options.
3 In the Category list, select **Remote Info**	
From the Access list, select **Local/Network**	
In the Remote root folder box, select the Remote site subfolder	In the current unit folder.
4 Check **Enable file check in and check out**	
5 Check **Check out files when opening**	
	(If necessary.) To set Dreamweaver to check out files automatically when you open them.
6 Enter your name in the Check out name box	(Enter either your name or a fake name.) This is what other users see when you check out files.
7 Click **OK**	To define the site.
8 Double-click **index.html**	A dialog box appears asking if you want to include dependent files, such as images or style sheets.
Click **No**	A second dialog box appears asking if you want to overwrite your local copy of the file.
Click **No**	To close the dialog box and open the page. In the Files panel, a green check mark appears next to the file, indicating that you've checked it out.

9 Place the insertion point after the second paragraph in the center column

   Type **Order your copy online today!**

> This recipe is available in our book, *Outlander Cooking!* Order your copy online today!|

To add another sentence to the content.

10 Save and close index.html

Although you closed the file, it's still checked out. You have to check in files before others can open them.

11 In the Files panel, select index.html

If necessary.

At the top of the panel, click 🔒

(The Check In button.) A dialog box appears asking if you want to check in dependent files. Because the changes you made to the page were textual, you don't need to check in dependent files.

Click **No**

To check the file back in. A lock icon is now visible next to the file. You won't be able to edit the file until you check it out again.

Design notes

Explanation

Sometimes in group settings, you might want to attach notes to files so that others can understand the changes you made to a file or know what changes still need to be made. You can communicate with other project members by attaching Design Notes to files.

To create a design note:

1   Open the file to which you want to attach a Design Note.

2   Choose File, Design Notes to open the Design Notes dialog box, shown in Exhibit 8-3.

3   From the Status list, select a status option for the note.

4   If you want to add the current date to the note, click the small date icon on the right side.

5   In the Notes box, enter the note you want for the file.

6   If you want users to see the note when they open the file, check Show when file is opened.

7   Click OK to create the note.

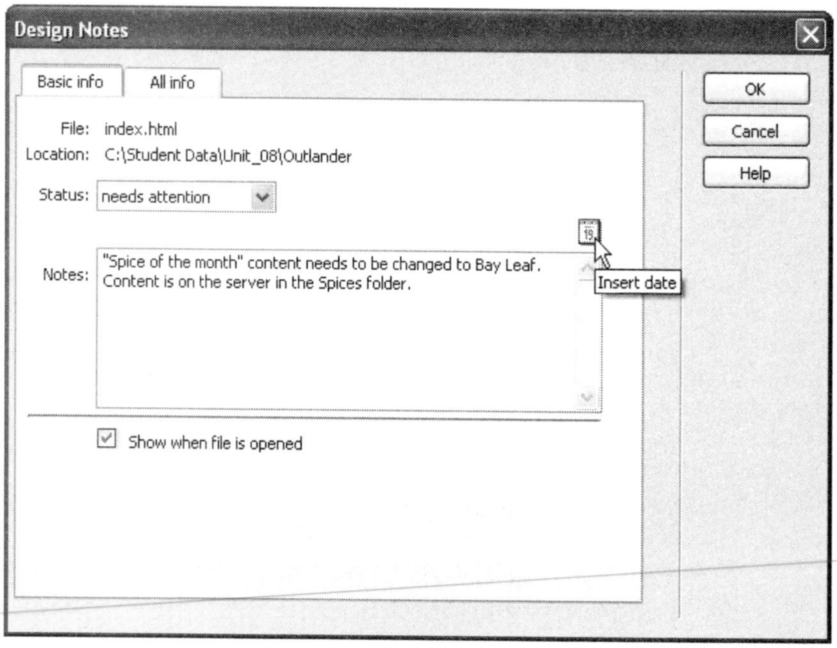

Exhibit 8-3: The Design Notes dialog box

If you opted to show the note when the file opens, the Design Notes dialog box appears whenever the file opens, even if you work on the file and save it again. If this option isn't selected, users must choose File, Design Notes to preview the notes attached to the file.

Do it!

A-2:   Adding a Design Note

Here's how	Here's why
1 Open index.html	Dreamweaver automatically checks the file out again.
Click **No**	To close the dependent files alert box.

2	Choose **File, Design Notes...**	To open the Design Notes dialog box.
	From the Status list, select **needs attention**	
3	Click the date icon	

To add today's date to the note.

	Click beneath the date, then type **"Spice of the month" content needs to be changed to Bay Leaf. Content is on the server in the Spice folder.**	

4	Check **Show when file is opened**	
	Click **OK**	To close the dialog box.
5	Close index.html	You'll check to make sure that the note appears when someone opens the file.
	Open index.html	The Design Notes dialog box appears, showing the note you created.
	Click **Cancel**	To close the dialog box.
	Close index.html	
6	Choose **Site, Manage Sites...**	To open the Manage Sites dialog box.
	Verify that **Outlander collaboration** is selected	
	Click **Edit**	To open the Site Definition dialog box.
7	Under Category, select **Remote Info**	
	Clear **Enable file check in and check out**	To disable the check in/check out options.
	Click **OK**	To close the Site Definition dialog box.
8	Click **Done**	To close the Manage Sites dialog box.

Topic B: Compatibility testing

This topic covers the following Adobe ACE exam objective for Dreamweaver CS3.

#	Objective
3.13	List and describe, and resolve issues related to, browser compatibility.

Check Browser Compatibility

Explanation

Users are likely to visit your Web site by means of a variety of browsers and browser versions. Some browsers are less standards-compliant than others, and many older browsers can produce inconsistent results when certain development techniques are used. You should always check to make sure that your pages appear as intended in the most commonly used browsers. You should also be sure that your content is accessible to users with older, less standards-compliant browsers, as well as users with special devices, such as screen readers and Braille printers.

Dreamweaver's Check Browser Compatibility feature makes it easier to identify and fix potential browser compatibility issues. The feature tests the HTML, CSS, and JavaScript code in your documents against your target browsers (the browsers that you want to test for compatibility with your site.) When you run Check Browser Compatibility, the Results panel displays any errors and warnings. This report can save you time in your efforts to ensure compatibility with a variety of browsers.

To run a manual check on a single document:

1 Open the document.

2 Click the Check Page button and choose Check Browser Compatibility to open the Results panel.

3 In the Results panel, click Check Browser Compatibility. The Results panel displays the name of the document, the specific lines of code that contain problems, and a description of each problem, as shown in Exhibit 8-4. It also displays an icon that indicates the severity of each problem, as follows:

   • A red exclamation point to indicate an error.

   • A yellow exclamation point to indicate a warning.

   • A word-balloon to indicate a message.

Exhibit 8-4: The Browser Compatibility Check panel in the Results panel group

The Check Browser Compatibility feature isn't perfect and shouldn't be the only method you use to test your pages prior to publishing. It's a good idea first to use Check Browser Compatibility for all target browsers, and then to test your pages in the browsers themselves to double-check consistency of design, layout, and functionality.

Do it!   ## B-1: Checking for browser-specific errors

Here's how	Here's why
1 Open gallery.html	(From the Files panel.) You'll check this document for browser-specific problems.
2 In the Document toolbar, click [Check Page]	To display the Check Page menu.
Choose **Settings...**	To display the Target Browsers dialog box.
Verify that all browsers are checked	
Click **OK**	
3 Click [Check Page]	
Choose **Check Browser Compatibility**	
4 In the Results toolbar, click [▷] and choose **Check Browser Compatibility**	To run the browser compatibility check against the current page.
Observe the panel	There are no issues with the current browser settings.
5 Click [▷] and choose **Settings...**	To open the Target Browsers dialog box.
Click the list next to Netscape	The minimum browser versions include only the current version and a few recent versions. Early versions of a browser, such as Netscape 4.0, aren't supported.
Click the list next to Internet Explorer and select **5.0**	

☑	Firefox	2.0 ▾
☑	Internet Explorer	5.0 ▾
☑	Internet Explorer for Macintosh	5.0
☑	Netscape	5.5
☑	Opera	6.0
☑	Safari	7.0
		2.0 ▾

	You'll check compatibility with this earlier version of Internet Explorer.
Click **OK**	To close the dialog box.
6 Observe the Results panel	A warning about an unsupported property appears.
Observe the information in the Browser Support Issue box	The issue and the browser it affects are listed.

7 On the right side of the Results panel, click	(The Options menu.) To display the menu options for the panel group.
Choose **Open Results in Browser**	To open the report in the default browser. The page lists the browsers targeted and any issues that resulted from the Browser Compatibility Check.
Close the browser	
8 Set **6.0** as the minimum browser version of Internet Explorer	Open the Target Browsers dialog box from the document toolbar or the Results panel, then select 6.0 from the list beside Internet Explorer, and click OK.
9 Right-click the Results panel group tab	
Choose **Close panel group**	To close the Results panel group.
10 Close gallery.html	
11 What are the minimum browser versions that you typically develop for, and why?	

Topic C: Accessibility

This topic covers the following Adobe ACE exam objective for Dreamweaver CS3.

#	Objective
2.7	List and describe the features Dreamweaver provides for Accessibility Standards/Section 508 compliance.

Section 508

Explanation

As you create sites, it's important to keep in mind that some people don't use conventional browsers, such as Internet Explorer and Firefox. For example, users with visual impairments often use screen readers to access Web site content.

Section 508 of the U.S. Rehabilitation Act prohibits federal agencies from buying, developing, maintaining, or using electronic and information technologies that are inaccessible to people with disabilities. Sites that comply with Section 508 are accessible to a variety of devices, such as audio readers (which read Web site content aloud), Braille printers, and screen magnifiers for the visually impaired. Although the law extends only to federal agencies, it's always good to try and design your pages so that they're accessible to the largest audience possible.

Every effort you make to ensure that your content is accessible also helps ensure that your content is accessible to other devices, such as cell phones, PDAs, and future technologies. Developing pages that are accessible can also help build a loyal user base.

WCAG guidelines

To help make your pages accessible, you can design them based on Section 508 guidelines and Web Content Accessibility Guidelines (WCAG). The WCAG guidelines are organized into three categories: Priority 1, Priority 2, and Priority 3. The Priority 1 category includes guidelines that designers must satisfy in order for their sites to be considered accessible.

The Priority 2 category includes guidelines designers should address to help ensure that their sites are accessible to a wider variety of readers. The Priority 3 category includes guidelines designers could address, if they want to improve access further to their content. You can use Dreamweaver to check pages against Priority 1 and Priority 2 guidelines.

To check a page for accessibility:

1 Open the page you want to check.

2 Choose Site, Reports to open the Reports dialog box.

3 Under HTML Reports, check Accessibility.

4 Click Report Settings to open the Accessibility dialog box, shown in Exhibit 8-5. By default, all accessibility guidelines are enabled.

5 To disable a group of guidelines, select the group, then click Disable. You can also disable individual guidelines by expanding the group, selecting the guideline, and clicking Disable.

6 Click OK to close the dialog box.

7 Click Run to check the page.

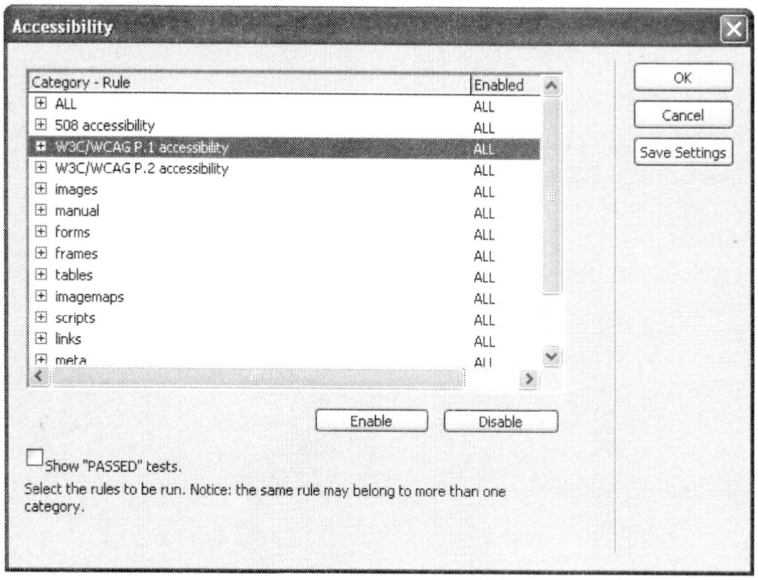

Exhibit 8-5: The Accessibility dialog box

Fixing accessibility issues

When you check pages or sites for accessibility issues, the results automatically display in the Site Reports panel, as shown in Exhibit 8-6. Some issues are marked with a question mark icon. This indicates that the page didn't fail the accessibility test, but you should check to make sure that the accessibility requirement is fulfilled correctly. For example, for images that contain ALT text, you should check to make sure that the text adequately describes the image instead of just providing its file name. If an issue displays a red x, you need to update the page to fulfill the requirement.

To check or fix issues, double-click the issue in the list. You can also obtain more information about the issue by selecting it and clicking the More Info button on the left side of the Site Reports panel.

More Info button

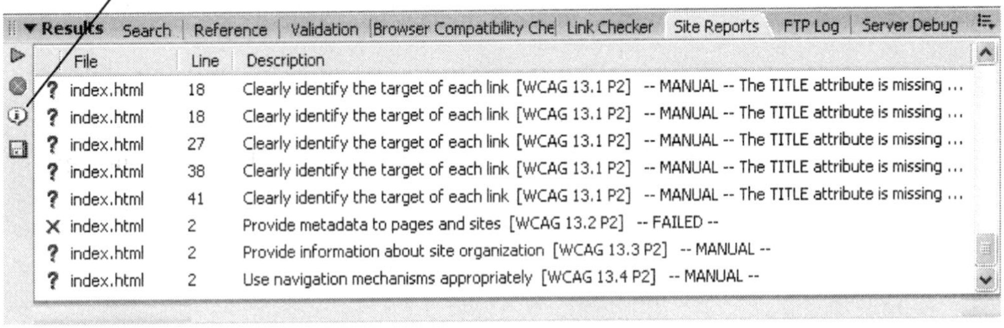

Exhibit 8-6: The Site Reports panel showing accessibility issues

Do it!

C-1: Checking accessibility

Here's how	Here's why
1 Open index.html	You'll check this document for potential accessibility problems.
Click **Cancel**	(If necessary.) To close the Design Notes dialog box.
2 Choose **Site**, **Reports...**	To open the Reports dialog box.
In the Report on list, verify that **Current Document** is selected	
Under HTML Reports, check **Accessibility**	
3 Click **Report Settings**	To open the Accessibility dialog box.
Observe the groups of guidelines	Within the list are Section 508 guidelines, as well as W3C/WCAG P.1 and P.2 guidelines.
Expand the W3C/WCAG P.1 group	
	(Click the plus sign to the left of the group.) To view the Priority 1 guidelines. You'll leave the default settings as they are.
4 Click **Cancel**	To return to the Reports dialog box.
5 Click **Run**	To check the page. The Results panel opens. The Site Reports tab activates and displays the Accessibility report.

6 Scroll to the top of the report list

   Click the first issue in the list

To select it. The issue indicates that non-spacer images should have ALT text. On the left side is a question mark icon, indicating that this might be something to take another look at, not that it failed to meet the requirements.

   Double-click the issue

The workspace changes to Split view, and the Spice of the month - turmeric image is selected. The logo has descriptive ALT text applied, so you don't need to fix anything.

7 Scroll to the bottom of the list

One issue is marked with a red x, indicating that it failed to meet accessibility requirements. All pages need to provide certain metadata in the head section. To fix this issue, you need to add metadata to the page.

8 Right-click the Results panel group tab, and choose **Close panel group**

To close the panel group.

9 Switch to Design view, and close index.html

Unit summary:Collaboration and publishing

Topic A   In this topic, you learned how to use the Check In/Check Out feature to manage files in a **group work setting**. You also attached a **Design Note** to a file to let coworkers know what changes needed to be made to a document.

Topic B   In this topic, you checked for **browser-specific errors** by using the Check Browser Compatibility feature and the Browser Compatibility Check tab in the Results panel.

Topic C   In this topic, you learned how to check for and fix **accessibility** problems using the Reports dialog box. You also observed accessibility issues in the Site Reports panel.

Independent practice activity

In this activity, you'll run a Target Browser Check on a Web page. Then you'll adjust the Target Browser Check settings to check for older versions of a browser.

1 Create a new site named **Collaboration practice**, using the Outlander folder inside the Practice subfolder as your local root folder. (*Hint*: Be sure to start with the current unit folder.)

2 Open products.html.

3 Perform a Browser Compatibility Check using the settings shown in Exhibit 8-7.

4 Review the error report and verify that no errors are found.

5 Close all open documents.

6 Open index.html.

7 Check the page for accessibility issues. (*Hint:* Choose Site, Reports to open the Reports dialog box.)

8 Fix the first accessibility issue. (*Hint:* The issue is that one of the images doesn't have any ALT text applied to it. Resolve the issue by adding ALT text.)

9 Save and close the document.

10 Close Dreamweaver.

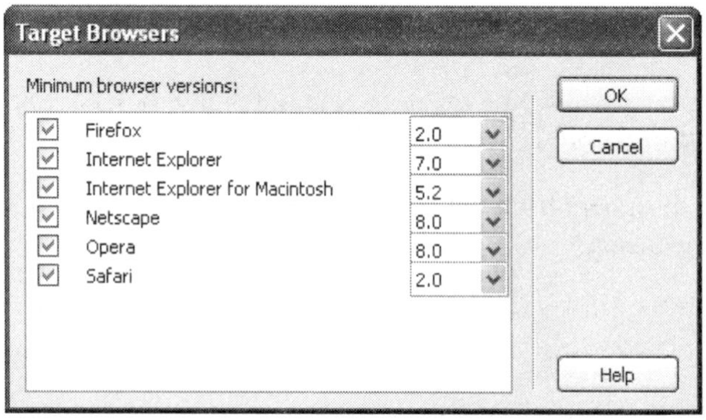

Exhibit 8-7: The Target Browser settings to apply at step 3

Review questions

1 Which is true about files checked out by another user? (Choose all that apply.)

  A Files checked out by another user have a red check mark next to them.

  B When you open a file checked out by another user, a dialog box appears asking if you want to incorporate their changes.

  C You can't edit files checked out by another user until they're checked back in.

  D When you open a file checked out by another user, it automatically becomes checked out to you, the current user.

2 Which is true about design notes? (Choose all that apply.)

  A In documents with design notes applied, the Design Note dialog box always appears when the document is opened.

  B When adding a design note, you can insert the current date by clicking the small date icon on the right side of the Design Note dialog box.

  C Documents with design notes applied appear with a small check next to them in the Files panel.

  D When adding a design note, you can select a status type from the Status list in the Design Note dialog box.

3 What are advantages of using the Check Browser Compatibility feature? (Choose all that apply.)

  A It allows you to check the HTML, CSS, and JavaScript code quickly in your documents against your target browsers.

  B The report it generates can save you time in your efforts to ensure compatibility with a variety of browsers.

  C It won't miss anything, so you don't have to worry about any browser support or compatibility problems if your page passes the test.

  D It corrects any problem code for you with the click of a button.

4 What does Section 508 of the U.S. Rehabilitation Act prohibit?

  A Web designers from developing, maintaining, or using information technology that's inaccessible to people with disabilities.

  B Web designers from developing e-commerce sites without the proper credentials and licensing.

  C Federal agencies from developing, maintaining, or using information technology that's inaccessible to people with disabilities.

  D Federal agencies from developing or maintaining sites which aren't accessible to all browsers.

5 Which WCAG guidelines should designers address to help ensure their sites are accessible?

   A Priority 1

   B Priority 2

   C Priority 3

   D Priority 4

6 How can you check for accessibility issues?

   A In the Document toolbar, click the Validate Markup button.

   B Choose Site, Reports. Under HTML Reports, check Accessibility, then click Run.

   C Choose Commands, Clean Up XHTML.

   D Right-click the Files panel, then choose Check Links Sitewide.

Appendix A

ACE exam objectives map

This appendix provides the following information:

A ACE exam objectives for Dreamweaver CS3 with references to corresponding coverage in ILT Series courseware.

Topic A: ACE exam objectives

Explanation

The following table lists the Adobe Certified Expert (ACE) exam objectives for Dreamweaver CS3 and indicates where each objective is covered in conceptual explanations, hands-on activities, or both.

#	Objective	Course level	Conceptual information	Supporting activities
1.1	Given an HTML tag, explain the purpose of that tag. (Tags include: <div> <span> <table> <a>.)	Basic	Unit 1, Topic D	D-1
1.2	Describe the difference between CSS classes and IDs.	Basic	Unit 3, Topic C	C-1
		Advanced	Unit 1, Topic B	B-5
1.3	Explain how JavaScript is used on the client in Web pages.	Advanced	Unit 4, Topic A	A-1
1.4	List and describe the features and functionality of ftp and how it is used in Dreamweaver.	Basic	Unit 7, Topic B	B-1
2.1	Define a local site by using the Manage Sites dialog box.	Basic	Unit 7, Topic A	A-1
2.2	Manage site definitions for local, remote, and testing server information.	Basic	Unit 2, Topic A	A-1
2.3	Describe considerations related to case-sensitive links.	Basic	Unit 7, Topic A	A-1
2.4	Given a scenario, define the structure of a site.	Basic	Unit 2, Topic A	A-1
2.5	Given a scenario, select and set the appropriate resolution for a site.	Basic	Unit 2, Topic B	B-1
2.6	List and describe considerations related to designing a site for multiple platforms and browsers.	Basic	Unit 1, Topic C Unit 2, Topic A Unit 7, Topic A Unit 7, Topic B	C-5 A-1 A-1
2.7	List and describe the features Dreamweaver provides for Accessibility Standards/Section 508 compliance.	Basic	Unit 1, Topic C Unit 4, Topic A Unit 5, Topic A	C-4 A-1 A-3
		Advanced	Unit 3, Topic B Unit 8, Topic C	B-2 C-1
2.8	Explain how templates are used to architect for reuse and consistency.	Advanced	Unit 2, Topic C	C-1, C-2
2.9	Create pages by using CSS starter pages.	Basic	Unit 2, Topic B Unit 3, Topic C	 C-1

#	Objective	Course level	Conceptual information	Supporting activities
2.10	Explain how to extend Dreamweaver by using Extensions.	Advanced	Unit 4, Topic B	B-4
2.11	Given a scenario, set development Preferences.	Basic	Unit 1, Topic C Unit 2, Topic A Unit 2, Topic B Unit 3, Topic A	 A-1 A-1
2.12	Given a scenario, choose the proper method to lay out a page. (Methods include: tables, layers, CSS Box model.)	Basic Advanced	Unit 4, Topic A Unit 1, Topic B Unit 3, Topic A Unit 5, Topic A	 B-1 A-1 A-1
3.1	List and describe how to navigate the Dreamweaver UI.	Basic	Unit 1, Topic B	B-1 thru B-3
3.2	Use Find and Replace including support for regular expressions.	Basic	Unit 1, Topic A	A-1
3.3	Create and use page templates.	Advanced	Unit 2, Topic C	C-1, C-2
3.4	Create and maintain Cascading Style Sheets (CSS.)	Basic Advanced	Unit 3, Topic C Unit 6, Topic C Unit 1, Topic A Unit 1, Topic B	C-1 thru C-5 C-1 A-1 B-2 thru B-5
3.5	Create and use reusable page objects by using library items.	Advanced	Unit 2, Topic A	A-1, A-2
3.6	Explain the purpose of and how to use Server-side includes.	Advanced	Unit 2, Topic B	B-1, B-2, B-3
3.7	Create and use code Snippets.	Advanced	Unit 2, Topic A	A-1
3.8	Given a method, lay out a page. (Methods include: Table Layout, Layers, Expanded Tables mode.)	Basic Advanced	Unit 4, Topic A Unit 4, Topic D Unit 5, Topic A Unit 5, Topic B	A-1 D-1, D-2, D-3 A-1 B-1, B-2, B-3
3.9	List and describe the options for creating and saving new pages.	Basic	Unit 2, Topic B	B-1
3.10	Set document properties by using the Document Properties dialog box.	Basic	Unit 2, Topic B	B-3, B-4
3.11	Lay out a page by using guides.	Advanced	Unit 5, Topic A	A-1
3.12	List and describe the options available for formatting the structure of a document. (Options include: paragraph breaks, line breaks, non-breaking spaces, tables.)	Basic	Unit 3, Topic A Unit 4, Topic A Unit 4, Topic B	A-1, A-2 A-1, A-2 B-2
3.13	List and describe, and resolve issues related to, browser compatibility.	Advanced	Unit 8, Topic B	B-1, B-2

#	Objective	Course level	Conceptual information	Supporting activities
3.14	Use JavaScript behaviors to implement page functionality. (Behaviors include: Pop-Up Menus, Open Browser Window, Swap Image, Go To URL.)	Advanced	Unit 4, Topic B	B-1, B-2, B-3
3.15	Add Flash elements to a Web page. (Options include: text, buttons, video, paper.)	Advanced	Unit 6, Topic A Unit 6, Topic B	A-1, A-2 B-1, B-2, B-3
3.16	List and describe the functionality provided by Dreamweaver for XML.	Advanced	Unit 7, Topic A Unit 7, Topic B	A-1, A-2 B-1, B-2, B-3
3.17	Given a coding tool or feature, describe the purpose of or how to use that tool or feature. (Tools or features include: Code and Design View, Code Collapse, Code Navigation, Code Hinting, Coding Context Menu option.)	Basic Advanced	Unit 1, Topic D Unit 3, Topic A Unit 4, Topic A	D-1 A-2 A-1
3.18	Discuss considerations related to naming conventions and case sensitivity (e.g., variations between UNIX and Windows.)	Basic	Unit 7, Topic A Unit 7, Topic B	A-1
3.19	Annotate files by using Design Notes and Comments	Advanced	Unit 8, Topic A	A-2
4.1	Manage collaboration with multiple developers by using Check In-Check Out.	Advanced	Unit 8, Topic A	A-1
4.2	List and describe the different methods for accessing a remote site. (Methods include: FTP, LAN, VSS, WebDAV.)	Basic	Unit 7, Topic B	B-1
4.3	Given an access method, configure site definitions.	Basic	Unit 7, Topic B	B-1
4.4	Transfer and synchronize files to and from a remote server. (Options include: Cloaking, background file transfer, Get, Put.)	Basic	Unit 7, Topic A Unit 7, Topic B	A-3 B-2, B-3
4.5	Manage assets, links, and files for a site.	Basic	Unit 7, Topic B	B-3
4.6	Configure preferences, and explain the process required to compare files.	Basic Advanced	Unit 7, Topic B Unit 8, Topic A	B-3
4.7	Validate a site prior to deployment (Options include: link checking, accessibility checking, validating markup.)	Basic Advanced	Unit 7, Topic A Unit 8, Topic C	A-3, A-4 C-1

Course summary

This summary contains information to help you bring the course to a successful conclusion. Using this information, you'll be able to:

A Use the summary text to reinforce what you've learned in class.

B Determine the next courses in this series, if any, as well as any other resources that might help you continue to learn about Dreamweaver CS3.

Topic A: Course summary

Use the following summary text to reinforce what you've learned in class.

Unit summaries

Unit 1

In this unit, you learned how **HTML** and **CSS** work together, and identified the difference between **internal** and **external style sheets**. You created and attached an external style sheet to a page. You learned about **the <div> tag**, and how to **define content sections** to establish a page layout. Lastly, you created and applied **ID styles** and modified CSS rules.

Unit 2

In this unit you created and manipulated **library items**, **snippets**, **server-side includes**, and page **templates** in order to quickly update site pages. You also discussed the use of **head elements**, edited an existing head element, and added **keywords** and a **site description** to a page's head section.

Unit 3

In this unit, you created an **interactive form**. You added and edited form **input fields**, such as **text fields**, **textarea fields**, **lists**, **menus**, **check boxes**, and **radio buttons**. You also learned how to enhance the **accessibility** of forms by defining a logical **tab order**.

Unit 4

In this unit, you learned about **rollover images**. You created a **navigation bar** with rollovers, and you used the **Swap Image behavior** to control other images on the page. Then you applied the **Open Browser Window behavior** to open a new browser window when users click a link, and you learned how to download Dreamweaver **extensions**.

Unit 5

In this unit, you learned how to work with **AP Divs**. You inserted AP Divs using the Draw AP Div tool, and added content. You also learned how to **select**, **name**, **resize**, and **position** AP Divs. You learned that any absolutely positioned element is displayed in the **AP Elements panel**, and you learned how to **dynamically control layer visibility** by applying the Show-Hide Elements behavior.

Unit 6

In this unit, you added and modified **Flash buttons** and **Flash text**. You also added **Flash files**, **FlashPaper**, and **Windows Media Player** and **QuickTime** movie files. Lastly, you learned how to create a basic **timeline animation** in the Timeline Panel.

Unit 7

In this unit, you learned how to **convert an HTML page to an XSLT page**. You referenced an XML document in **the Bindings panel**, and used the schema to add **XML placeholders** within the XSLT page. You also created a **repeat region** in the XSLT page. Finally, you **created dynamic links**, and attached an XSLT page to an XML document.

Unit 8

In this unit, you learned how to **check in** and **check out** a file, attach a **Design Note** to a file, and **check for browser-specific errors** using the Check Browser Compatibility feature. Finally, you learned how to check for and **fix accessibility problems** by using the Reports dialog box.

Topic B: Continued learning after class

It's impossible to learn to use any software effectively in a single day. To get the most out of this class, you should begin working with Dreamweaver CS3 to perform real tasks as soon as possible. We also offer resources for continued learning.

Next courses in this series

This is the last course in this series.

Other resources

For more information, visit www.axzopress.com.

D r e a m w e a v e r   C S 3 :   A d v a n c e d

Quick reference

Button	Shortcut keys	Function
		Hides the panel groups and expands the document window.
▽	CTRL + TAB	Expands the Property inspector.
▼		Hides the Property inspector and expands the document window.
I	CTRL + I	Applies the italic style to the selected text.
🌐	F12	Previews the current page in the default browser.
Split		Splits the Document window into Code view and Design view.
Code		Changes the Document window to Code view.
Design		Changes the Document window to Design view.
		Expands and collapses the Files panel.
		Attaches an External Style Sheet to the current page.
		Inserts a div tag.
All		Displays all style sheet files in the CSS panel.
✏		Edits an existing CSS style in the CSS panel.
		Creates a new CSS style in the CSS panel.
		Creates a Spry Menu Bar.

Button	Shortcut keys	Function
CSS	SHIFT + F11	Displays the current style sheet files in the CSS panel, or opens the CSS panel from the Property inspector.
	CTRL + ALT + T	Inserts an HTML table.
B	CTRL + B	Applies the bold format to the selected text.
		Activates the Library section of the Assets panel.
		Creates a new library item.
		Edits a library item.
		Creates a new snippets folder in the Snippets panel.
		Creates a new Server-side include.
		The Templates button.
		Resets a modified image to its original size and proportions.
	F5	Refreshes a view or list in a panel.
		Displays the meta data in a Web page.
		Displays the page title in a Web page.
		Displays the CSS style sheet linked to a Web page.
		Inserts a new form on the page.
		Inserts a text field in a form.
		Inserts a textarea field in a form.
		Inserts a list box in a form.
		Inserts a check box in a form.
		Inserts a radio button in a form.
		Inserts a Submit or Reset button in a form.

Button	Function
⊞	Adds navigation items to the Nav bar elements list in the Insert Navigation Bar dialog box.
▲	Moves navigation items up in the Nav bar elements list in the Insert Navigation Bar dialog box.
+▾	Adds a behavior to the Behaviors panel.
⊟	Draws an AP Div on a page.
⚘ ▾	Inserts a Flash button on a Web page.
⟳	Creates a Repeat Region on an xslt page.
⌂	Checks in files.
☰▾	Displays options for a panel group.

Glossary

AP Div

A generic container that you can use to define content sections or contain content for any purpose. AP Divs are absolutely positioned <div> tags.

Assets

Components of your Web site, such as images or multimedia files.

Cascading Style Sheets (CSS)

The standard style language for the Web. While HTML provides the basic structure of a page, CSS controls how the elements within that structure appear in a browser.

Check box

A form input field that allows a user to select multiple items or indicate a yes/no or on/off selection.

Div

A division, or generic container (a <div> tag), that you can use for a variety of purposes.

External style sheet

An external text file that's saved with a .css extension and that contains style rules that define how various HTML elements display.

Flash button

An SWF file consisting of four frames. The first three frames define the button states, which correspond to the link, hover (rollover), and active states of an HTML link. The fourth frame of the movie defines the hotspot for the button image.

Flash text

An SWF file that allows you to apply special fonts that your users might not have installed on their computers. You can also use a Flash text if you want to create a variety of text effects that aren't available with standard font sets.

FlashPaper

Special SWF files created from a PDF version of the original document by using Macromedia FlashPaper 2. With FlashPaper, you can embed a standard word processing document or other document type into a Web page.

Layer

Another name for an AP Div.

Library

A special Dreamweaver file you can use to store assets, such as images, tables, sound files, and video files, for your Web pages.

List/Menu

A form input field that displays a list from which the user can select one or more items.

Media-dependent style sheet

A style sheet containing code that directs browsers or other media devices to specific rules within the sheet.

Meta tags

Tags in the head section that provide information about the page's content, such as keywords and a description. Meta tags also specify page properties, such as character encoding, the author, or copyright information.

Pop-up menu

A menu in which additional navigational links appear when you point to one of the root links.

Radio button

A form input field that allows a user to select only one item from a list of items.

Rollover

A popular technique in which an image is replaced by another image when a user points to it or clicks it. This type of interactivity is popular, because it provides visual feedback for a user's actions.

Server-side includes

Similar to library items, they're maintained by the server after you upload a site. They provide an efficient way to update pages without having to make the changes manually and then re-upload the pages.

Snippets

Similar to library items, except that they can't be updated universally throughout a site. However, they allow you to add code that you would normally have to type repeatedly, such as code for <div> containers or navigation bars.

Swap image

An action that uses a trigger object to cause changes to one or more other images on a page. The trigger object itself doesn't change.

Tab order

The order in which the insertion point jumps from input field to input field as the user presses the Tab key.

Template

A document you can create and apply to other site pages in order to maintain consistency and make the site maintenance process faster and easier.

Template expression

A variable or parameter established in a template that allows you to use the template in various ways. For example, you can use template expressions to show or hide certain optional areas in the template, depending on a condition that you set up.

Textarea field

A form input field that accepts longer text entries, for such things as user feedback, support questions, and posts in a message board forum.

Text field

A form input field that accepts a single word or short phrase, such as a name or address.

XML (Extensible Markup Language)

A structured language that organizes document components as data, so you can reuse the content in a variety of formats

XSLT (Extensible Stylesheet Language Transformations)

A subset of XSL that lets you display XML data on a page and transform the data into HTML. You create XSLT pages, and then use them like templates to control page layout.

Index